Mathematics for Schools
an integrated series
Level II Book 5

Senior Authors	Assistant Author	Contributing Authors	
Harold Fletcher	Ruth Walker	Kathleen Minikin	John S. Moon
Arnold Howell		John Page	Gwyn D. Price
		John C. Walters	Jack Wood

 ADDISON-WESLEY PUBLISHERS LIMITED

London · Reading, Massachusetts

This book is in the Addison-Wesley series Mathematics for Schools
Level I for 5–7 year olds
Level II for 7–13 year olds

Teacher's Resource Book for Level II, Books 5 and 6 (SBN 201 02119 6)
Suggestions for the *vital* Preliminary Activities, which should precede the use of the children's books, are contained in the *Teacher's Resource Book*.
There are also comments on the pages of the children's books, and suggestions for Follow-up Activities and Enrichment Activities.

For contents see back of book.

Illustrated by: Design Practitioners Ltd.
                            Channell Purkis Llewellyn
Cover photograph: Donald Pittman

ISBN 0 201 02138 2

Section 1 · Bases

POSITION VALUE: DIFFERENT BASES

Tom matches ten marbles with his ten fingers and arranges a set of ten.

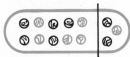

He records: 1 set of ten and 3 units $\xrightarrow{\text{can be written as}}$ 13
He says: "There are thirteen marbles."

Betty matches five marbles with five fingers and arranges sets of five.

She records: 2 sets of five and 3 units $\longrightarrow 23_{five}$
She says: "There are two three, base five, marbles."

Tom says: "I used base ten. I could have recorded 1 ten and 3 units as 13_{ten}. I could have said there are one three, base ten, marbles."

1 Record in base ten the total number of marbles in each set.

2 Record in base five the total number of marbles in each set above.

3 Draw pictures to illustrate each of these recordings.

a] 32_{five}	b] 18_{ten}	c] 43_{five}	d] 43_{ten}	e] 32_{four}
f] 24_{five}	g] 24_{ten}	h] 24_{six}	i] 10_{five}	j] 22_{three}
k] 23_{four}	l] 22_{five}	m] 21_{six}	n] 12_{six}	o] 11_{two}

4 Draw some objects. Record the totals in base five.

POSITION VALUE: DIFFERENT BASES

Dick arranges his marbles in sets of five. He draws a picture of the marbles. Using base five, he records the total and illustrates it on an abacus.

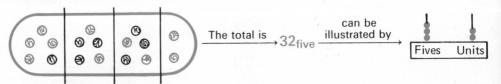

The total is $\rightarrow 32_{five} \xrightarrow{\text{can be illustrated by}}$

| Fives | Units |

1 Using Dick's method, draw pictures and illustrate on an abacus each of these recordings.

a] 21_{three} b] 21_{four} c] 41_{five} d] 14_{six} e] 27_{eight}

f] 31_{seven} g] 25_{six} h] 10_{eight} i] 20_{three} j] 14_{five}

$24_{five} \xrightarrow{\text{can be arranged as}} 2$ sets of five and 4 units

2 Complete.

a] $34_{eight} \longrightarrow \square$ sets of ▦ and △ units

b] $43_{eight} \longrightarrow \square$ sets of ▦ and △ units

c] $46_{seven} \longrightarrow \square$ sets of ▦ and △ units

d] $54_{six} \longrightarrow \square$ sets of ▦ and △ units

e] $24_{five} \longrightarrow \square$ sets of ▦ and △ units

f] $24_{six} \longrightarrow \square$ sets of ▦ and △ units

---

4 sets of 5 and 3 units $\xrightarrow{\text{can be written as}} 43_{five}$

3 Complete.

a] 5 sets of 7 and 2 units $\longrightarrow \square$ b] 4 sets of 6 and 3 units $\longrightarrow \square$
c] 7 sets of 9 and 4 units $\longrightarrow \square$ d] 3 sets of 4 and 0 units $\longrightarrow \square$
e] 2 sets of 3 and 1 unit $\longrightarrow \square$ f] 1 set of 3 and 2 units $\longrightarrow \square$

---

4 Complete the matrix by counting on.

Base ten	5	6	7	8	9	10	11	12	13	14	15	16	17	18
Base nine	5	6	7	8	10									
Base eight	5	6	7											
Base seven	5	6	10											
Base six	5	10	11											

2

POSITION VALUE: DIFFERENT BASES

Judy records in base four the total number of her marbles.

3 sets of four and 3 units —can be written as→ 33_{four}

She now wins another marble.

She says: "I can exchange four sets of four for one set of four fours, that is for one set of sixteen."

She records: 1 set of sixteen, 0 sets of four, and 0 units —can be written as→ 100_{four}

1 Complete.

a] $22_{three} + 1_{three}$ ——→ $\square_{three}$ b] $44_{five} + 1_{five}$ ——→ $\square_{five}$

c] $55_{six} + 1_{six}$ ——→ $\square_{six}$ d] $66_{seven} + 1_{seven}$ ——→ $\square_{seven}$

Judy wins six more marbles.
She records: Six can be arranged as 1 set of four and 2 units ——→ 12_{four}
She says: "Altogether I have 1 set of sixteen, 1 set of four, and 2 units."
She records: 1 set of sixteen, 1 set of four, and 2 units —can be written as→ 112_{four}

2 Complete.

a] 212_{four} ——→2 sets of $\square$, 1 set of $\triangle$, and 2 units

b] 212_{three} ——→2 sets of $\square$, 1 set of $\triangle$, and 2 units

c] 212_{five} ——→2 sets of $\square$, 1 set of $\triangle$, and 2 units

---

Ann illustrates 123_{four} on an abacus. 123_{four} —can be illustrated by→

Sixteens (four fours)	Fours (four units)	Units

3 Illustrate each of these numbers on an abacus.

a] 213_{four} b] 321_{four} c] 213_{four} d] 513_{six} e] 351_{six}

f] 212_{three} g] 422_{five} h] 324_{five} i] 143_{eight} j] 256_{seven}

k] 110_{two} l] 304_{five} m] 340_{five} n] 211_{three} o] 100_{six}

4 Write some numerals in different bases. Illustrate each numeral on an abacus.

5 Play the Exchange Game.

3

ADDITION INVOLVING EXCHANGE

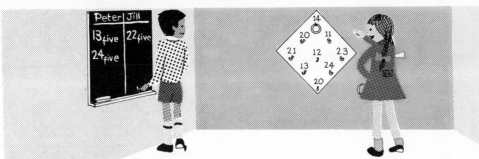

Peter and Jill play each other at base five hoop-la. Both children want to find their total scores.

Peter uses five-pieces and unit-pieces.

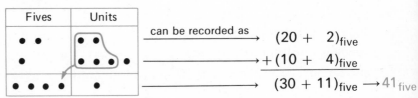

can be recorded as → $(10 + 3)_{five}$

→ $+ (20 + 4)_{five}$

→ $(30 + 12)_{five} \rightarrow 42_{five}$

Peter's score is 42_{five}.

Jill uses a counting board.

Fives	Units
• •	• •
•	• • • •
• • •	•

can be recorded as → $(20 + 2)_{five}$

→ $+ (10 + 4)_{five}$

→ $(30 + 11)_{five} \rightarrow 41_{five}$

Jill's score is 41_{five}.

1   Use Peter's method to find these total scores for base five hoop-la.

a] 11_{five} b] 22_{five} c] 13_{five} d] 23_{five} e] 14_{five} f] 23_{five}

   $+14_{five}$ $+13_{five}$ $+14_{five}$ $+12_{five}$ $+24_{five}$ $+14_{five}$

2   Use Jill's method to find these total scores for base six hoop-la.

a] 22_{six} b] 13_{six} c] 33_{six} d] 24_{six} e] 15_{six} f] 11_{six}

   $+25_{six}$ $+25_{six}$ $+14_{six}$ $+12_{six}$ $+15_{six}$ $+35_{six}$

3   Find the missing bases for each of these.

a] $3_\square + 2_\square = 10_\square$ b] $4_\square + 1_\square = 10_\square$ c] $31_\square + 4_\square = 40_\square$

d] $24_\square + 4_\square = 32_\square$ e] $33_\square + 5_\square = 42_\square$ f] $23_\square + 3_\square = 32_\square$

g] $12_\square + 2_\square = 21_\square$ h] $56_\square + 6_\square = 65_\square$ i] $17_\square + 5_\square = 24_\square$

4   Write some scores using different bases. Record each total.

4

ADDITION INVOLVING EXCHANGE

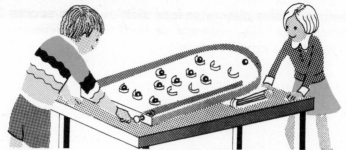

Sam and Rita play each other at base three bagatelle. Both children want to find their total scores.

Sam 1st turn: 121_{three} Rita 1st turn: 112_{three}

2nd turn: 21_{three} 2nd turn: 22_{three}

Sam uses nine-pieces, three-pieces, and unit-pieces.

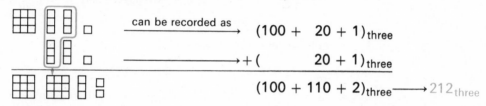

can be recorded as $\longrightarrow$ $(100 + 20 + 1)_{three}$

$\longrightarrow + (\qquad 20 + 1)_{three}$

$(100 + 110 + 2)_{three} \longrightarrow 212_{three}$

Sam's score is 212_{three}.

Rita uses a counting board.

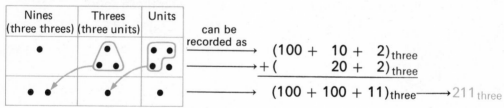

Nines (three threes)	Threes (three units)	Units

can be recorded as $\longrightarrow$ $(100 + 10 + 2)_{three}$

$\longrightarrow + (\qquad 20 + 2)_{three}$

$\longrightarrow (100 + 100 + 11)_{three} \longrightarrow 211_{three}$

Rita's scores is 211_{three}.

1 Use any method to find these total scores.

a] 121_{three} b] 123_{four} c] 213_{five} d] 131_{five} e] 112_{four}

  $+\ 12_{three}$ $+101_{four}$ $+124_{five}$ $+222_{five}$ $+132_{four}$

f] 345_{six} g] 253_{seven} h] 467_{eight} i] 467_{nine} j] 467_{ten}

  $+122_{six}$ $+134_{seven}$ $+156_{eight}$ $+156_{nine}$ $+156_{ten}$

2 Play the Base Game.

COMPARISON: DIFFERENT BASES

Joan and John play base four skittles. Joan scores 331_{four} points and John scores 112_{four} points. Joan finds the difference between their scores using a counting board.

Sixteens (four fours)	Fours (four units)	Units
● ● ● ●	● ● ● 	●
●	●	● ●

can be recorded as → $(300 + 30 + 1)_{four}$
→ $-(100 + 10 + 2)_{four}$

So that she can compare units with units, Joan exchanges 1 four for 4 units. Now she has one one, base four, units.

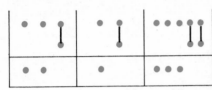

can be recorded as → $(300 + 20 + 11)_{four}$
→ $-(100 + 10 + 2)_{four}$
→ $(200 + 10 + 3)_{four} → 213_{four}$

John finds the difference by counting on.

$112_{four} \xrightarrow{+3_{four}} 121_{four} \xrightarrow{+10_{four}} 131_{four} \xrightarrow{+200_{four}} 331_{four}$

To 112_{four} he added $(3 + 10 + 200)_{four} = 213_{four}$ in order to count on to 331_{four}

The difference between the scores is 213_{four}.

1 Use any method to find the difference between these scores.

a] 221_{three}
-110_{three}

b] 323_{four}
-111_{four}

c] 212_{four}
-113_{four}

d] 441_{five}
-213_{five}

e] 324_{five}
-142_{five}

f] 411_{five}
-234_{five}

g] 544_{six}
-151_{six}

h] 421_{six}
-154_{six}

i] 512_{six}
-355_{six}

j] 625_{seven}
-432_{seven}

k] 630_{seven}
-415_{seven}

l] 701_{ten}
-263_{ten}

m] 601_{seven}
-465_{seven}

n] 622_{eight}
-477_{eight}

o] 603_{eight}
-214_{eight}

2 Find the missing bases for each of these.

a] $12_\square - 3_\square = 9_\square$

b] $12_\square - 3_\square = 4_\square$

c] $23_\square - 14_\square = 9_\square$

d] $23_\square - 14_\square = 4_\square$

e] $22_\square - 14_\square = 4_\square$

f] $42_\square - 35_\square = 4_\square$

g] $32_\square - 23_\square = 3_\square$

h] $21_\square - 12_\square = 2_\square$

i] $21_\square - 12_\square = 4_\square$

3 Play the Missing Base Game.

Section 2 · Statistics

COLLECTING AND STUDYING DATA

Paul collects this data about one Friday's television programmes.

News:	13.45–13.50	Comedy: 18.00–18.30	For children: 13.25–13.45
	17.50–18.00	20.00–20.30	16.20–17.50
	21.00–21.30	20.30–21.00	Other: 13.00–13.25
	22.40–22.45	Films: 18.45–20.00	18.30–18.45
For schools:	09.40–11.35	Plays: 13.50–14.05	22.45–23.15
	14.05–14.25	21.30–22.40	23.15–23.50

1 Find the total viewing time for each kind of programme.

a] Plays   b] Films   c] For children   d] For schools
e] Comedy   f] News   g] Other

2 Record on a bar chart the data about the viewing times.

3 Which kind of programme occupied:

a] the most viewing time?   b] the least viewing time?

4 What is the difference in time between the two times in Exercise 3?

5 Collect data about one Saturday's television programmes. Record on a bar chart the data about the viewing times using the same headings as for Friday's programmes.

6 Which kind of programme occupied:

a] the most viewing time?   b] the least viewing time?

7 What is the difference in time between the two times in Exercise 6?

8 Write about the differences you notice between Friday's and Saturday's programmes.

COLLECTING AND STUDYING DATA

Study this article which Carol cut out of the newspaper.

TELEVISION *by Ivor Sett*

LAST NIGHT's *Vista* from LTV celebrated the visit of the President to the rapidly expanding lunar settlement. It took the opportunity to examine man's achievements there since the first moon landing twenty-five years ago. Coverage of the event opened with a live extra-terrestrial broadcast from the control cabin of the module "Lunaria" as the President personally took the controls in the final minutes before touchdown. After the usual welcoming speeches, the President chaired a discussion by international experts about lunar occupation and exploration. Here, at last, the programme really began to get to grips with the problems with which the moon presents us. The opinions of our own Professor Malcolm Stanley lent much weight to the view that the planet should be handed over to the United Nations once and for all.

1
a] Estimate which letter of the alphabet occurs most frequently.
b] Record on a tally chart the total number of times each letter occurs.
c] Now record your data on a bar chart.
d] Was your estimate about which letter would occur most frequently correct ?
e] Record in order the six most frequently occurring letters.
f] Do you think the same six letters will always occur most frequently in any newspaper article ?

We call the number of times a letter occurs, the frequency.

2 From any newspaper, cut out a short article of about ten lines. Using this article, repeat Exercise 1.

3 Compare your results for Exercises 1 and 2. Write about what you notice.

4 Ask your teacher for a newspaper or a book in a foreign language.

a] Using about ten lines of print, repeat Exercise 1.
b] Write about what you notice.

5 In setting type for a newspaper or a book:

a] which six letters would be needed most ?
b] which three letters would be needed least ?

INTRODUCING THE MEDIAN

The height of each of these children has been measured to the nearest centimetre. They have arranged themselves in height order from the shortest to the tallest.

Jim	Ann	Tom	Bill	Sue	John	Mary
119 cm	124 cm	132 cm	136 cm	138 cm	145 cm	150 cm

1 Which child is:

a] the tallest? **b]** the shortest? **c]** in the middle of the group?

2 What is the height of the child in the middle of the group?

We call the height of the child in the middle the median height of the 7 children.

The mass of each of these children has been measured to the nearest kilogramme.

Jim	Ann	Tom	Bill	Sue	John	Mary
36 kg	37 kg	41 kg	40 kg	44 kg	43 kg	46 kg

3 Arrange the children's masses in order from the least to the greatest.

4 **a]** Which child has the median mass? **b]** What is the median mass?

Bob, who is 151 cm tall and has a mass of 49 kg, joins the 7 children. The children rearrange themselves in height order. Because there is now an even number of children, no child is in the middle of the group.

5 **a]** Now which 2 children are nearest to the middle of the group?
b] What are their heights?
c] What is the height half way between these two heights?

The half way height is 137 cm because

$$138 - 136 = 2 \text{ and } \tfrac{2}{2} = 1 \text{ so } 136 + 1 = 137$$

We call 137 cm the median height of the 8 children.

6 Find the median mass of the 8 children.

INTRODUCING THE MEDIAN

The children have had their shoe sizes measured in the shop.

Jim	Ann	Tom	Bill	Bob	John	Mary
$4\frac{1}{2}$	4	5	6	7	7	$6\frac{1}{2}$

1   Arrange the children's shoe sizes in order from the smallest to the largest.

2   What is the median shoe size?

3   Sue who has a shoe size of $5\frac{1}{2}$ now joins her friends.

    a] Now which two shoe sizes are nearest to the middle?
    b] What is the median shoe size?
    c] Could you buy a shoe with this size?

4   For 5 of your friends:

    a] measure the height of each to the nearest centimetre.
    b] measure the mass of each to the nearest kilogramme.
    c] find the shoe size of each.

5   For your 5 friends what is:

    a] the median height?   **b]** the median mass?   **c]** the median shoe size?

6   Ask one of your friends to measure:

    a] your height.   **b]** your mass.   **c]** your shoe size.

7   When you join your 5 friends what is the new:

    a] median height?   **b]** median mass?   **c]** median shoe size?

8   Write down the median value for each of these sets.

    a] {8, 9, 10, 11, 12, 13, 14}   **b]** {8, 9, 10, 11, 12, 13}
    c] {8, 9}   **d]** {1·0, 0·8, 1·2, 1·1, 0·9}
    e] {7 kg, 5 kg, 2 kg, 8 kg, 9 kg, 11 kg}   **f]** $\{\frac{1}{2}, \frac{3}{4}, \frac{1}{4}, \frac{3}{8}, \frac{7}{8}\}$
    g] {1·5 m, 70 cm, $\frac{1}{2}$ m, 125 cm, $\frac{3}{4}$ m, 80 cm}

INTRODUCING THE ARITHMETIC MEAN

Ian, Dave, and Lucy each measured the length of their span to the nearest centimetre. They recorded their results.

	Ian	Dave	Lucy
Length of span	16 cm	17 cm	12 cm

Ian says: "The length of the median span is 16 cm."
Lucy says: "If we put our spans together, we could stretch across (16 + 17 + 12) cm = 45 cm. There are three of us and 3(15) = 45 and (15 + 15 + 15) = 45. If we each had a span of 15 cm, we could just stretch across the same length, 45 cm."

We say 15 is the arithmetic mean of 16, 17, and 12.

1 Complete the open sentences.

a] $4 + 6 + 11 = \square \xrightarrow{\text{can be written as}} 3(\triangle) = \square \xrightarrow{\text{can be written as}} \triangle + \triangle + \triangle = \square$
The mean of 4, 6, and 11 is $\triangle$.

b] $4 + 9 + 8 = \square \longrightarrow 3(\triangle) = \square \longrightarrow \triangle + \triangle + \triangle = \square$
The mean of 4, 9, and 8 is $\triangle$.

c] $5 + 7 + 12 = \square \longrightarrow 3(\triangle) = \square \longrightarrow \triangle + \triangle + \triangle = \square$
The mean of 5, 7, and 12 is $\triangle$.

d] $12 + 8 = \square \longrightarrow 2(\triangle) = \square \longrightarrow \triangle + \triangle = \square$
The mean of 12 and 8 is $\triangle$.

e] $3 + 6 + 8 + 11 = \square \longrightarrow 4(\triangle) = \square \longrightarrow \triangle + \triangle + \triangle + \triangle = \square$
The mean of 3, 6, 8, and 11 is $\triangle$.

f] $12 + 15 + 13 + 12 = \square \longrightarrow 4(\triangle) = \square \longrightarrow \triangle + \triangle + \triangle + \triangle = \square$
The mean of 12, 15, 13, and 12 is $\triangle$.

2 Here are the stride lengths of the 3 children:

Ian——→60 cm, Dave——→70 cm, Lucy——→56 cm.

a] What is the median stride length? **b]** What is the mean stride length?

3 Here are the foot lengths of 4 other children:

Jack——→21 cm, Dan——→24 cm, Sally——→17 cm, Mandy——→18 cm.

a] What is the median foot length? **b]** What is the mean foot length?

4 Find both the median and the mean of:

a] 4, 7, and 13. **b]** 4 and 10. **c]** 5, 6, 10, and 15. **d]** 3 and 6.

5 Write about what you notice in Exercise 4.

11

ASSIGNMENT: MEDIAN AND MEAN

1   Measure to the nearest centimetre your stride length and your foot length.

2   **a**] Repeat Exercise 1 for 6 of your friends.
      b] Record in order of size the stride lengths.
      c] Record in order of size the foot lengths.

3   Record on separate bar charts the data about:

      a] the stride lengths.   **b**] the foot lengths.

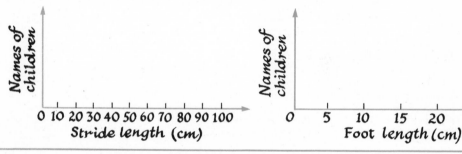

4   **a**] What is the length of the median stride? Mark this in red on your bar chart.
      b] Calculate the length of the mean stride. Mark this in blue on your bar chart.
      c] What is the length of the median foot length? Mark this in red on your bar chart.
      d] Calculate the length of the mean foot length. Mark this in blue on your bar chart.

5   Find the difference between:

      a] the median and mean stride.   **b**] the median and mean foot length.

6   Write about anything else you notice on your bar charts.

7   Repeat Exercises 1–5 using the length of the span instead of the stride and the distance round the head instead of the foot length.

Section 3 · Addition and Difference

INTRODUCING THOUSANDS

In the match factory, 100 matches are packed in a box. Then 10 boxes are packed in a carton.
We say: "Ten sets of one hundred is one thousand."
We write 10 sets of 1 hundred as 1000.

1 Complete the matrix.

Sets of one hundred	20	30	40	50	60	70	80	90	100
Sets of one thousand	2								
Numeral	2000								

2 Record each number illustrated in these four different ways.

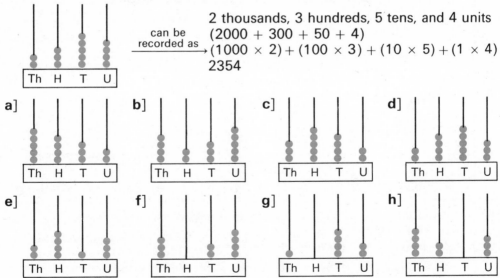

2 thousands, 3 hundreds, 5 tens, and 4 units
can be recorded as (2000 + 300 + 50 + 4)
$(1000 \times 2) + (100 \times 3) + (10 \times 5) + (1 \times 4)$
2354

a] Th H T U
b] Th H T U
c] Th H T U
d] Th H T U

e] Th H T U
f] Th H T U
g] Th H T U
h] Th H T U

3 Illustrate each number on a separate abacus.

a] 2563 b] 5036 c] 6003 d] 7030 e] 8136 f] 9345 g] 4962
h] 4127 i] 3156 j] 4307 k] 6021 l] 3520 m] 2971 n] 8703

POSITION VALUE

D	C	B	A

At the football ground, there are 10 spectators in each row. There are 10 rows in each section and 10 sections in each block.

1 How many spectators are:

a] in 1 row?　　**b**] in 3 rows?　　**c**] in 5 rows?　　**d**] in 10 rows?
e] in 1 section?　**f**] in 3 sections?　**g**] in 5 sections?　**h**] in 10 sections?
i] in 1 block?　　**j**] in 3 blocks?　　**k**] in 5 blocks?　　**l**] in 10 blocks?

2 Complete the matrix.

Number of spectators	Number of full blocks	Number of full sections	Number of full rows
1420	1	14	142
3560			
7829			
6023			
9870			

3 Illustrate, then record each number in this way.

Th	H	T	U

4316 ──can be illustrated by──→ [dots diagram] ──contains──→ 4316 units
431 tens
43 hundreds
4 thousands

a] 5621　**b**] 2516　**c**] 1625　**d**] 6152　**e**] 3563　**f**] 7049　**g**] 4907

4 Arrange the numbers in order from the greatest to the least.
a] 1987, 2346, 1678, 5004, 999, 4291, 3058, 2634.
b] 3706, 3076, 3760, 3067, 3607, 3670, 3707, 3570.
c] 5781, 5178, 8751, 1578, 1758, 3785, 2857, 4583.

5 For each of the numbers in Exercise 4 record the number that is:
a] ten more.　**b**] one hundred more.　**c**] one thousand more.

6 Play the Thousands Game.

ADDITION INVOLVING EXCHANGE

4516 spectators watched Rovers play City and 3758 watched Rangers play Albion. What was the total attendance for both games?

Pam uses her counting board to find the sum.

Th	H	T	U
●●	● ●	●	●●
●●	● ●		●●
● ●	●●● ●	● ●	●●●
	●● ●	● ●	●●
●●● ●	●●●●● ●●●●	●●● ●	●●●● ●●●● ●●

can be recorded as → (4000 + 500 + 10 + 6)

──────→ + (3000 + 700 + 50 + 8)

──────→ (7000 + 1200 + 60 + 14)

Because the units column has more than 9 units and the hundreds column has more than 9 hundreds, she exchanges 10 units for 1 ten and 10 hundreds for 1 thousand.

●●● ●● ●●	●●	●●● ●	●●
8	2	7	4

──────→ (8000 + 200 + 70 + 4)──────→8274

Ken finds the sum using these methods.

4516   can be   (4000 + 500 + 10 + 6)   or   4516
+3758 ─written as─→ + (3000 + 700 + 50 + 8)   +3758
                      ──────────────────────   ────
                      (7000 + 1200 + 60 + 14)──────→8274   14
                                                                      60
                                                                    1200
                                                                    7000
                                                                    ────
                                                                    8274

8274 people watched the two games.

1 Use Pam's or one of Ken's methods to find the total attendances.

a] 2173	b] 5923	c] 1568	d] 3682	e] 1927
+5494	+3716	+5214	+1695	+3849

f] 2867	g] 3592	h] 3652	i] 834	j] 4987
1965	5449	2348	5276	3765
+3987	+ 965	+3001	+3765	+1998

k] 1546	l] 945	m] 1693	n] 4975	o] 6097
7372	6783	7324	836	2376
+ 796	+2009	+ 461	+1987	+1412

2 Play the "9000 Up" Game.

ADDITION INVOLVING EXCHANGE

This table shows the distances in kilometres by air between some of the cities in the world.

	San Francisco	Tokyo	Sydney	Delhi	Lagos	Buenos Aires	New York
London	8616	9590	17,019	6732	5003	11,135	5538
New York	4152	10,858	16,011	11,755	8447	8534	
Buenos Aires	10,404	18,351	11,766	15,796	7939		
Lagos	12,554	13,486	15,525	8077			
Delhi	12,379	5858	10,433				
Sydney	11,948	7818					
Tokyo	8285						

1 Use the data in the table to find the total distance in kilometres for each of these flights:

a] London to New York to San Francisco.
b] London to Lagos to Delhi.
c] London to Sydney to Tokyo.
d] London to Buenos Aires to New York.
e] New York to Lagos to Sydney.
f] Tokyo to London to San Francisco.
g] Delhi to New York to Tokyo.
h] Buenos Aires to Lagos to Tokyo.
i] Buenos Aires to Tokyo to Delhi to London.
j] San Francisco to Buenos Aires to Delhi to Sydney.

2 Find the total distance in kilometres for each of these flights.

a] 3671 km +1263 km	**b]** 6923 km +2467 km	**c]** 8888 km +6341 km	**d]** 4365 km +3297 km
e] 6349 km +5718 km	**f]** 4932 km +8163 km	**g]** 3996 km +2771 km	**h]** 9291 km +8764 km
i] 3271 km 6492 km +1876 km	**j]** 4941 km 5623 km +1814 km	**k]** 7766 km 5542 km +3178 km	**l]** 9164 km 4527 km +8134 km

COMPARISON INVOLVING EXCHANGE

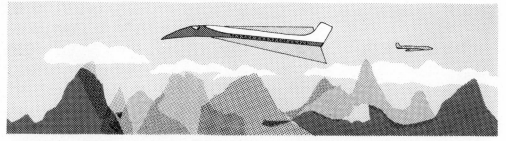

Julie flew 4152 km from New York to San Francisco and Peter flew 8616 km from London to San Francisco. How much farther did Peter fly?

Julie finds the difference using a counting board.

Th	H	T	U
•••••••••• •••••	•		••••••
••••	•	•••••	••

can be recorded as →

$(8000 + 600 + 10 + 6)$
$- (4000 + 100 + 50 + 2)$

So that she can compare tens with tens, Julie exchanges 1 hundred for 10 tens. Now she has 11 tens.

→ $(8000 + 500 + 110 + 6)$
→ $- (4000 + 100 + 50 + 2)$
→ $(4000 + 400 + 60 + 4) \rightarrow 4464$

Peter finds the difference using this method.

$$\begin{array}{r} 8616 \\ -4152 \end{array} \rightarrow \begin{array}{r} (8000 + 600 + 10 + 6) \\ -(4000 + 100 + 50 + 2) \end{array} \rightarrow \begin{array}{r} (8000 + 500 + 110 + 6) \\ -(4000 + 100 + 50 + 2) \\ \hline (4000 + 400 + 60 + 4) \rightarrow 4464 \end{array}$$

Peter flew 4464 km farther than Julie.

1 Using the table on page 16, find the difference in distance in kilometres between each of these flights:

a] Delhi to London and Delhi to New York.
b] Lagos to Sydney and Delhi to Sydney.
c] Tokyo to Lagos and Tokyo to Delhi.
d] Lagos to New York and Lagos to Buenos Aires.
e] Delhi to Buenos Aires and Delhi to Lagos.
f] San Francisco to London and San Francisco to New York.
g] Tokyo to London and Tokyo to New York.
h] Sydney to London and Sydney to New York.
i] Tokyo to New York and Tokyo to Buenos Aires.
j] London to Sydney and Tokyo to Buenos Aires.

2 Play the "9000 Down" Game.

COMPARISON INVOLVING COUNTING ON

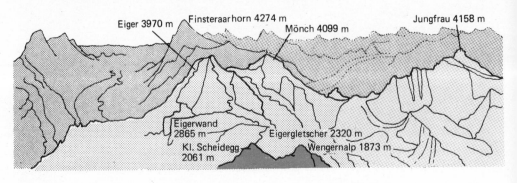

Eiger 3970 m   Finsteraarhorn 4274 m   Mönch 4099 m   Jungfrau 4158 m

Eigerwand 2865 m   Eigergletscher 2320 m   Wengernalp 1873 m   Kl. Scheidegg 2061 m

1   Arrange the heights in order from the highest to the lowest.

Molly finds the difference in height between Jungfrau and Wengernalp using this method.

$$1873 \xrightarrow{+27} 1900 \xrightarrow{+100} 2000 \xrightarrow{+2158} 4158$$

To 1873 she adds (27 + 100 + 2158) = 2285 and reaches 4158.

The difference between the height of Jungfrau and Wengernalp is 2285 m.

2   Use Molly's method to find the difference in height between:

a] Mönch and Eigergletscher.   b] Eiger and Kl. Scheidegg.
c] Finsteraarhorn and Wengernalp.   d] Jungfrau and Eigerwand.
e] Eiger and Wengernalp.   f] Eigerwand and Eigergletscher.
g] Mönch and Eiger.   h] Jungfrau and Kl. Scheidegg.
i] Finsteraarhorn and Eiger.   j] Eiger and Eigerwand.
k] Mönch and Eigergletscher.   l] Jungfrau and Eiger.

Here are the lengths of some rivers in kilometres.

Lena 4480; Loire 1005; Yukon 3166; Darling 1904;
Snake 1661; Mackenzie 4022; Amazon 6241; Danube 2832.

3   Find the differences in length between each of these pairs of rivers:

a] Loire and Lena.   b] Yukon and Snake.
c] Mackenzie and Amazon.   d] Loire and Yukon.
e] Lena and Mackenzie.   f] Danube and Snake.
g] Snake and Amazon.   h] Loire and Amazon.
i] Yukon and Mackenzie.   j] Darling and Lena.
k] Danube and Amazon.   l] Amazon and Darling.
m] Mackenzie and Danube.   n] Lena and Amazon.

ENRICHMENT

The garage hires out cars. Every three months, they record the reading on the odometer of each car.

1 Complete the matrix, showing how many kilometres each car has travelled in each three month period.

Registration number	UMT985K	KHX374L	BLM604L	FYT538K	SOL886M	JTO168M
January 1st (km)	1961	3836	2874	3678	3987	2419
March 31st (km)	7892	8592	7438	9421	6422	6084
Distance travelled (km)	5931					
April 1st (km)	7892	8592	7438	9421	6422	6084
June 30th (km)	13,019	14,670	12,813	16,509	12,392	13,771
Distance travelled (km)	5127					

2 Complete the matrix, showing how many kilometres each car has travelled from January 1st to June 30th.

Registration number	UMT985K	KHX374L	BLM604L	FYT538K	SOL886M	JTO168M
Distance travelled (km)						

3 Using the data in the matrix, calculate the distance travelled by each driver on:

a] the first day. b] the second day. c] the third day. d] the total journey.

	Smith	Gray	Brown	Scott	Ross	Jones
Start (km)	1864	6429	10,031	23,821	3334	15,630
End of 1st day (km)	2350	6787	10,470	24,292	3810	16,079
End of 2nd day (km)	2639	7126	10,989	24,511	4226	16,835
End of 3rd day (km)	3008	7519	11,422	24,902	4715	17,338

4 Check each of your results in Exercises 2 and 3 using a different method.

Section 4 · Fractions

FRACTIONS AS PART OF A UNIT

Don wants to solve this problem: "Half of the boys in the set are eating ice-cream. The number of the boys eating ice-creams is three. How many boys are in the set?"

Because half of the boys are eating ice-creams, the set has been partitioned into two equivalent subsets.

Don draws pictures and records.

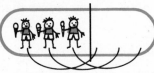 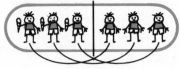

Number of members in the subset ⟶ 3
Fraction of members of the set that are in the subset ⟶ $\frac{1}{2}$
Number of members in the set ⟶ 6

1 Use Don's method to complete the matrix.

Number of members in subset	4	4	3	6	10	6	12	12	7	21
Fraction of members of set that are in subset	$\frac{1}{2}$	$\frac{1}{3}$	$\frac{1}{4}$	$\frac{2}{3}$	$\frac{2}{5}$	$\frac{1}{8}$	$\frac{3}{4}$	$\frac{3}{5}$	$\frac{1}{10}$	$\frac{3}{10}$
Number of members in set	8									

2 Write a story to illustrate each of the first three examples in Exercise 1.

This is half of the area of a unit shape.

The whole of the area of the unit shape might look like this.

or   or

3 Using centimetre squared paper, copy each of these half unit shapes. For each shape, draw 3 different whole unit shapes.

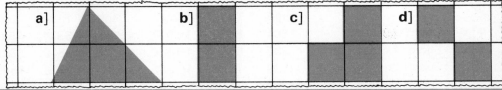

a]   b]   c]   d]

4 Repeat Exercise 3 using each shape as a quarter unit shape instead of a half unit shape.

20

EQUIVALENT FRACTIONS

Lynn shades in part of the area of the unit shape. She writes two different fraction names for the part of the area she has shaded.

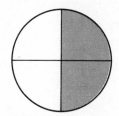

She writes: $\frac{2}{4} = \frac{1}{2}$

$\frac{1}{2}$ and $\frac{2}{4}$ are equivalent fractions.

1 Use the shaded part of each of these unit shapes to record pairs of equivalent fractions.

a]  b] c]   d]

2 Draw, then shade a unit shape to illustrate each of these pairs of equivalent fractions.

a] $\frac{4}{8}$ and $\frac{1}{2}$ b] $\frac{4}{6}$ and $\frac{2}{3}$ c] $\frac{3}{3}$ and $\frac{6}{6}$ d] $\frac{2}{10}$ and $\frac{1}{5}$

e] $\frac{3}{6}$ and $\frac{1}{2}$ f] $\frac{6}{10}$ and $\frac{3}{5}$ g] $\frac{4}{5}$ and $\frac{8}{10}$ h] $\frac{5}{10}$ and $\frac{1}{2}$

Lynn discovers that $\frac{1}{2}$, $\frac{2}{4}$, $\frac{3}{6}$, $\frac{4}{8}$, $\frac{5}{10}$ are all equivalent fractions. She could go on finding more fractions equivalent to $\frac{1}{2}$.

$\{\frac{1}{2}, \frac{2}{4}, \frac{3}{6}, \frac{4}{8}, \frac{5}{10}, \ldots\}$ is a family of equivalent fractions.

We call it an equivalence class.

Each member of the class represents the same number $\frac{1}{2}$.
We write . . . after $\frac{5}{10}$ to show that we can go on finding more members of the family.

The name of the family $\{\frac{1}{2}, \frac{2}{4}, \frac{3}{6}, \frac{4}{8}, \frac{5}{10}, \ldots\}$ is $\frac{1}{2}$.

3 Write four members of the family of equivalent fractions for each of these family names. Drawing pictures may help you.

a] $\frac{1}{3}$ b] $\frac{1}{4}$ c] $\frac{2}{3}$ d] $\frac{1}{5}$ e] $\frac{2}{5}$ f] $\frac{1}{10}$ g] $\frac{1}{6}$ h] $\frac{5}{6}$

We can represent $\frac{1}{2}$, $\frac{2}{4}$, and $\frac{3}{6}$ on a number line. They are all represented by the same point A.

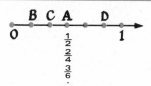

4 Name three fractions for: a] point B. b] point C. c] point D.

EQUIVALENT FRACTIONS

$\{\frac{1}{1}, \frac{2}{2}, \frac{3}{3}, \frac{4}{4}, \frac{5}{5}, \frac{6}{6}, \ldots\}$ is a family of equivalent fractions.
The name of the family is 1.

1 Write down five more members of the family of 1.

Jean wants to find other fractions equivalent to $\frac{1}{2}$. She knows that when she multiplies a number by 1, the value is unchanged:

$$2 \times 1 = 2, \quad 1 \times 1 = 1, \text{ and } \frac{1}{2} \times 1 = \frac{1}{2}.$$

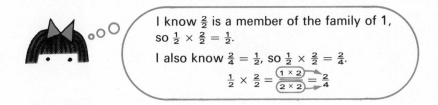

I know $\frac{2}{2}$ is a member of the family of 1, so $\frac{1}{2} \times \frac{2}{2} = \frac{1}{2}$.

I also know $\frac{2}{4} = \frac{1}{2}$, so $\frac{1}{2} \times \frac{2}{2} = \frac{2}{4}$.

$$\frac{1}{2} \times \frac{2}{2} = \frac{(1 \times 2)}{(2 \times 2)} = \frac{2}{4}$$

Jean has discovered how to multiply by a member of the family of 1.
She can use her discovery to find other fractions equivalent to $\frac{1}{2}$:

$$\frac{1}{2} \times \frac{3}{3} = \frac{3}{6}; \quad \frac{1}{2} \times \frac{4}{4} = \frac{4}{8}; \quad \frac{1}{2} \times \frac{5}{5} = \frac{5}{10}.$$

$\frac{1}{2}, \frac{2}{4}, \frac{3}{6}, \frac{4}{8}, \frac{5}{10}$ are all equivalent fractions.

2 Use Jean's method to find the equivalent fractions.

a] $\frac{1}{2} \times \frac{6}{6} = \frac{\triangle}{\square}$ $\xrightarrow{\text{can be written as}}$ $\frac{1}{2} = \frac{\triangle}{\square}$

b] $\frac{1}{3} \times \frac{2}{2} = \frac{\triangle}{\square}$ $\longrightarrow$ $\frac{1}{3} = \frac{\triangle}{\square}$

c] $\frac{1}{4} \times \frac{2}{2} = \frac{\triangle}{\square}$ $\longrightarrow$ $\frac{1}{4} = \frac{\triangle}{\square}$

d] $\frac{1}{5} \times \frac{4}{4} = \frac{\triangle}{\square}$ $\longrightarrow$ $\frac{1}{5} = \frac{\triangle}{\square}$

e] $\frac{2}{5} \times \frac{2}{2} = \frac{\triangle}{\square}$ $\longrightarrow$ $\frac{2}{5} = \frac{\triangle}{\square}$

f] $\frac{3}{4} \times \frac{2}{2} = \frac{\triangle}{\square}$ $\longrightarrow$ $\frac{3}{4} = \frac{\triangle}{\square}$

3 Draw pictures to check that each pair of fractions in Exercise 2 are equivalent fractions.

4 Complete.

a] $\frac{1}{2} \times \frac{\square}{\square} = \frac{7}{14}$ b] $\frac{1}{3} \times \frac{\square}{\square} = \frac{3}{9}$ c] $\frac{2}{3} \times \frac{\square}{\square} = \frac{8}{12}$ d] $\frac{2}{3} \times \frac{\square}{\square} = \frac{\triangle}{15}$

e] $\frac{1}{2} \times \frac{\square}{\square} = \frac{\triangle}{8}$ f] $\frac{1}{5} \times \frac{\square}{\square} = \frac{\triangle}{10}$ g] $\frac{2}{3} \times \frac{\square}{\square} = \frac{4}{\boxed{}}$ h] $\frac{1}{6} \times \frac{\square}{\square} = \frac{5}{\boxed{}}$

LOWEST TERM FRACTIONS

Arnold and Harold are finding fractions equivalent to $\frac{4}{12}$.

Arnold  Because 2 is a factor of both 4 and 12, I can write

$$\frac{4}{12} = \frac{2 \times 2}{6 \times 2} = \frac{2}{6} \times \frac{2}{2}.$$

Because $\frac{2}{2}$ is a member of the family of 1, $\frac{4}{12} = \frac{2}{6}$.

Harold Because 4 is a factor of both 4 and 12, I can write

$$\frac{4}{12} = \frac{1 \times 4}{3 \times 4} = \frac{1}{3} \times \frac{4}{4}.$$

Because $\frac{4}{4}$ is a member of the family of 1, $\frac{4}{12} = \frac{1}{3}$.

We say 2 is a common factor of 4 and 12. We also say 4 is a common factor of 4 and 12.

1 Complete.

a] □ —is a common factor of→ 4 and 8   b] □ —is a common factor of→ 3 and 6

c] □ —————————→ 5 and 15   d] □ —————————→ 8 and 16

e] □ —————————→ 10 and 20   f] □ —————————→ 12 and 18

g] □ —————————→ 6 and 9   h] □ —————————→ 14 and 28

2 For each pair of numbers in Exercise 1, write down any other common factors you can find.

3 Use the children's method to find a fraction equivalent to each of these.

a] $\frac{4}{8}$ b] $\frac{3}{6}$ c] $\frac{5}{15}$ d] $\frac{10}{20}$ e] $\frac{12}{18}$ f] $\frac{6}{9}$ g] $\frac{3}{12}$ h] $\frac{4}{16}$

Look at the equivalence class $\{\frac{1}{3}, \frac{2}{6}, \frac{3}{9}, \frac{4}{12}, \ldots\}$.

For the fraction $\frac{4}{12}$, 4 and 12 —have as a common factor→ 4, 2, and 1.

$\frac{2}{6}$, 2 and 6 —————————→ 2 and 1.

$\frac{1}{3}$, 1 and 3 —————————→ 1.

Because 1 and 3 have no common factor other than 1, we call $\frac{1}{3}$ the lowest term member of this class.

$\frac{1}{3}$ is the lowest term fraction equivalent to $\{\frac{2}{6}, \frac{3}{9}, \frac{4}{12}, \ldots\}$.

4 Find the lowest term equivalent fraction for each of these.

a] $\frac{8}{12}$ b] $\frac{6}{10}$ c] $\frac{10}{16}$ d] $\frac{12}{16}$ e] $\frac{12}{24}$ f] $\frac{8}{24}$ g] $\frac{10}{24}$

h] $\frac{6}{9}$ i] $\frac{6}{15}$ j] $\frac{15}{20}$ k] $\frac{7}{21}$ l] $\frac{4}{8}$ m] $\frac{9}{15}$ n] $\frac{16}{20}$

5 Play the Fraction Domino Game.

ADDITION OF FRACTIONS

June and Tony look at these two families of fractions.

$$A \longrightarrow \{\tfrac{1}{2}, \tfrac{2}{4}, \tfrac{3}{6}, \tfrac{4}{8}, \ldots\} \qquad B \longrightarrow \{\tfrac{1}{3}, \tfrac{2}{6}, \tfrac{3}{9}, \tfrac{4}{12}, \ldots\}$$

$\tfrac{3}{6}$ in family A has numerator 3 and denominator 6.

$\tfrac{2}{6}$ in family B has numerator 2 and denominator 6.

June says: "$\tfrac{3}{6}$ and $\tfrac{2}{6}$ have the same denominator 6."

We say 6 is the common denominator of $\tfrac{3}{6}$ and $\tfrac{2}{6}$.

1 Record the next six fractions in: **a]** family A. **b]** family B.

2 Which is the next pair of fractions from family A and family B to have a common denominator?

3 **a]** Find a pair of fractions with a common denominator from these two families.

$$C \longrightarrow \{\tfrac{1}{2}, \tfrac{2}{4}, \ldots\} \qquad D \longrightarrow \{\tfrac{1}{5}, \tfrac{2}{10}, \ldots\}$$

b] Find the next two pairs.

June and Tony are discussing how to complete $\tfrac{1}{2} + \tfrac{1}{4} = \square$.

June says: "We could find the sum if both fractions had a common denominator."

She finds the lowest common denominator.

She records: $\tfrac{1}{2} \longrightarrow \{\tfrac{1}{2}, \tfrac{2}{4}, \tfrac{3}{6}, \tfrac{4}{8}, \ldots\} \quad \tfrac{1}{4} \longrightarrow \{\tfrac{1}{4}, \tfrac{2}{8}, \tfrac{3}{12}, \ldots\}$

$\tfrac{1}{2} + \tfrac{1}{4} \xrightarrow{\text{can be written as}} \tfrac{2}{4} + \tfrac{1}{4} = \tfrac{3}{4}$

She draws a picture to check her result.

Tony finds another common denominator.

He records: $\tfrac{1}{2} \longrightarrow \{\tfrac{1}{2}, \tfrac{2}{4}, \tfrac{3}{6}, \tfrac{4}{8}, \ldots\} \quad \tfrac{1}{4} \longrightarrow \{\tfrac{1}{4}, \tfrac{2}{8}, \tfrac{3}{12}, \ldots\}$

$\tfrac{1}{2} + \tfrac{1}{4} \xrightarrow{\text{can be written as}} \tfrac{4}{8} + \tfrac{2}{8} = \tfrac{6}{8} = \tfrac{3}{4}$

He draws a picture to check his result.

4 Use either June's or Tony's method to find the sums.

a] $\tfrac{1}{2} + \tfrac{1}{8} = \square$ **b]** $\tfrac{1}{3} + \tfrac{1}{6} = \square$ **c]** $\tfrac{1}{4} + \tfrac{1}{8} = \square$ **d]** $\tfrac{1}{10} + \tfrac{1}{5} = \square$

e] $\tfrac{1}{6} + \tfrac{1}{4} = \square$ **f]** $\tfrac{1}{2} + \tfrac{2}{5} = \square$ **g]** $\tfrac{1}{3} + \tfrac{2}{5} = \square$ **h]** $\tfrac{1}{4} + \tfrac{3}{8} = \square$

ADDITION OF FRACTIONS AND MIXED NUMBERS

Fred runs $\frac{3}{5}$ of a kilometre and walks $\frac{1}{2}$ of a kilometre. He wants to find out how far he has gone, $\frac{3}{5} + \frac{1}{2} = \square$.

He records: $\frac{3}{5} \longrightarrow \{\frac{3}{5}, \frac{6}{10}, \frac{9}{15}, \ldots\}$ $\frac{1}{2} \longrightarrow \{\frac{1}{2}, \frac{2}{4}, \frac{3}{6}, \frac{4}{8}, \frac{5}{10}, \ldots\}$

$$\frac{3}{5} + \frac{1}{2} = \frac{6}{10} + \frac{5}{10} = \frac{11}{10} = (\frac{10}{10} + \frac{1}{10}) = 1\frac{1}{10}$$

He finds he has gone $1\frac{1}{10}$ km.

1   Use Fred's method to complete the matrix.

Distance run (km)	$\frac{7}{10}$	$\frac{1}{2}$	$\frac{7}{10}$	$\frac{1}{2}$	$\frac{1}{4}$	$\frac{9}{10}$	$\frac{3}{10}$	$\frac{9}{10}$	$\frac{3}{4}$	$\frac{1}{2}$
Distance walked (km)	$\frac{1}{2}$	$\frac{3}{4}$	$\frac{4}{5}$	$\frac{4}{5}$	$\frac{9}{10}$	$\frac{3}{4}$	$\frac{1}{5}$	$\frac{4}{5}$	$\frac{3}{5}$	$\frac{2}{5}$
Total distance (km)	$1\frac{1}{5}$									

Joe runs $3\frac{3}{4}$ km and walks $2\frac{2}{5}$ km. He wants to find out how far he has gone, $3\frac{3}{4} + 2\frac{2}{5} = \square$.

He records: $\frac{3}{4} \longrightarrow \{\frac{3}{4}, \frac{6}{8}, \frac{9}{12}, \frac{12}{16}, \frac{15}{20}, \ldots\}$ $\frac{2}{5} \longrightarrow \{\frac{2}{5}, \frac{4}{10}, \frac{6}{15}, \frac{8}{20}, \ldots\}$

$$\begin{array}{r} 3\frac{3}{4} \\ + 2\frac{2}{5} \\ \hline \end{array} \text{ can be written as } \begin{array}{r} (3 + \frac{15}{20}) \\ + (2 + \frac{8}{20}) \\ \hline (5 + \frac{23}{20}) \end{array} \longrightarrow (5 + \frac{20}{20}) + \frac{3}{20} \longrightarrow 6\frac{3}{20}$$

He finds he has gone $6\frac{3}{20}$ km.

2   Use Joe's method to complete the matrix.

Distance run (km)	$3\frac{1}{2}$	$1\frac{7}{10}$	$2\frac{3}{5}$	$4\frac{3}{4}$	$3\frac{2}{5}$	$2\frac{1}{2}$	$3\frac{3}{10}$	$4\frac{1}{2}$	$2\frac{9}{10}$	$3\frac{7}{10}$
Distance walked (km)	$2\frac{3}{4}$	$1\frac{3}{5}$	$1\frac{1}{4}$	$2\frac{2}{5}$	$1\frac{1}{10}$	$2\frac{3}{5}$	$1\frac{2}{5}$	$2\frac{1}{4}$	$2\frac{2}{5}$	$1\frac{7}{10}$
Total distance (km)										

COMPARISON OF FRACTIONS AND MIXED NUMBERS

Going to school, Beth walks $\frac{7}{10}$ km and Kim walks $\frac{1}{2}$ km. The girls want to find out who walks the farther.

They record: $\frac{7}{10} \longrightarrow \{\boxed{\tfrac{7}{10}}, \tfrac{14}{20}, \tfrac{21}{30}, \ldots\}$ $\frac{1}{2} \longrightarrow \{\tfrac{1}{2}, \tfrac{2}{4}, \tfrac{3}{6}, \tfrac{4}{8}, \boxed{\tfrac{5}{10}} \ldots\}$

$\frac{7}{10} > \frac{5}{10}$ so Beth walks the farther.

The girls then want to find out how much farther Beth walks, $\frac{7}{10} - \frac{1}{2} = \square$.

They record: $\frac{7}{10} - \frac{1}{2} = \frac{7}{10} - \frac{5}{10} = \frac{2}{10} = \frac{1}{5}$

Beth walks $\frac{1}{5}$ km farther than Kim.

1 Use the girls' method to complete the matrix.

1st distance (km)	$\frac{7}{10}$	$\frac{5}{10}$	$\frac{1}{5}$	$\frac{3}{4}$	$\frac{2}{5}$	$\frac{3}{5}$	$\frac{9}{10}$	$\frac{7}{10}$	$\frac{3}{4}$	$\frac{4}{5}$
2nd distance (km)	$\frac{1}{4}$	$\frac{3}{4}$	$\frac{3}{10}$	$\frac{9}{10}$	$\frac{1}{2}$	$\frac{9}{10}$	$\frac{2}{5}$	$\frac{3}{4}$	$\frac{2}{5}$	$\frac{3}{4}$
Greater distance (km)	$\frac{7}{10}$	$\frac{3}{4}$								
Difference (km)	$\frac{9}{20}$									

Roger and Carl take part in a timed walk. When the time is up, Roger has walked $4\frac{2}{5}$ km and Carl has walked $2\frac{3}{4}$ km. The boys want to find out how much farther Roger walked, $4\frac{2}{5} - 2\frac{3}{4} = \square$.

They record: $\frac{2}{5} \longrightarrow \{\tfrac{2}{5}, \tfrac{4}{10}, \tfrac{6}{15}, \boxed{\tfrac{8}{20}} \ldots\}$ $\frac{3}{4} \longrightarrow \{\tfrac{3}{4}, \tfrac{6}{8}, \tfrac{9}{12}, \tfrac{12}{16}, \boxed{\tfrac{15}{20}} \ldots\}$

$$\begin{array}{c} 4\frac{2}{5} \\ -2\frac{3}{4} \end{array} \xrightarrow{\text{can be written as}} \begin{array}{c} (4 + \frac{8}{20}) \\ -(2 + \frac{15}{20}) \end{array} \xrightarrow{\text{can be written as}} \begin{array}{c} (3 + \frac{28}{20}) \\ -(2 + \frac{15}{20}) \\ \hline (1 + \frac{13}{20}) \longrightarrow 1\frac{13}{20} \end{array}$$

Roger walks $1\frac{13}{20}$ km farther than Carl.

2 Use the boys' method to complete the matrix.

1st distance (km)	$5\frac{1}{2}$	$7\frac{2}{5}$	$4\frac{7}{10}$	$2\frac{2}{5}$	$6\frac{1}{2}$	$3\frac{9}{10}$	$4\frac{1}{4}$	$5\frac{3}{5}$	$4\frac{2}{5}$	$8\frac{3}{10}$
2nd distance (km)	$1\frac{3}{4}$	$4\frac{9}{10}$	$2\frac{1}{2}$	$1\frac{1}{10}$	$4\frac{7}{10}$	$1\frac{3}{5}$	$2\frac{7}{10}$	$4\frac{4}{5}$	$3\frac{1}{4}$	$5\frac{7}{10}$
Difference (km)										

Section 5 · Measurement: Accuracy

MEASURING LENGTH ACCURATELY

You will need a metre trundle wheel, a metre rule, and a 20 m tape.

1 Using the trundle wheel, measure the length of your school hall or playground as accurately as you can. Measure the length three times.

Record each result.

Length of school hall		
1st:	2nd:	3rd:

2 a] Are each of your three results exactly the same?
b] If not, why do you think they are different?

3 Now measure the same length another three times using the metre rule. Record each result.

4 Measure the same length another three times using the tape. Record each result.

Jane measures the length of her school hall. She records her results.

	Length of school hall		
Using a trundle wheel	16½ m	17½ m	17m
Using a metre rule	16m 96 cm	17m 6 cm	17m 8 cm
Using a 20 m tape	17m 12 cm	17 m 8 cm	17m 10 cm

Jane says: "I cannot be certain what the accurate measurement of the length is. I think it must be greater than 16½ m and less than 17½ m."
She orders her nine results and records the median length, 17 m 8 cm.
She says: "I think that a fairly accurate measurement of the length is 17 m 8 cm, but there may be an error of a few centimetres, possibly 2 or 3 or even 4 or 5. I cannot be certain. I think that the length of the hall is between 17 m 3 cm and 17 m 13 cm."

5 Using Jane's method, make a fairly accurate measurement of your hall or playground from your results for Exercises 1, 3, and 4.

ESTIMATING ERRORS IN LENGTH

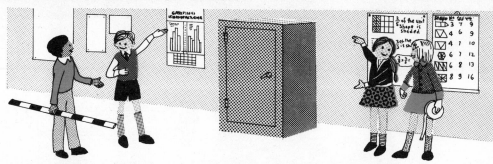

Bill and Ted are discussing how long the cupboard is. Bill says:
"I estimate the length to be greater than 150 cm and less than 180 cm.
I can calculate the median of my two estimates by finding the half way
distance between 150 cm and 180 cm.

$$180 - 150 = 30 \text{ and } \frac{30}{2} = 15 \text{ so } 150 + 15 = 165."$$

He checks his result: $165 + 15 = 180$ and $165 - 15 = 150$

Bill says: "I think that a fairly accurate estimate of the length of the
cupboard is 165 cm and it will probably not be in error by more
than 15 cm."

1 Look at a cupboard in the classroom. Use Bill's method to make a fairly
accurate estimate of its length.

2 Using a centimetre rule, measure as accurately as you can the length of
the cupboard. Do this twice. Repeat with a metre rule and with a tape
measure. Record your results.

Measurement of length of cupboard		
Using a centimetre rule	Using a metre rule	Using a tape measure
1st:	1st:	1st:
2nd:	2nd:	2nd:

3 Calculate the median length of: **a]** each pair of results. **b]** all six results.

4 Complete the sentences.

a] I think that a fairly accurate measurement of the length is □ cm.
b] The measurement will probably not be in error by more than △ cm.

5 Repeat Exercises 1–4 measuring the lengths of other objects in the
classroom.

6 Play the Error Game.

ESTIMATING ERRORS IN LENGTH

Mary says: "I estimate the length of my pencil to be greater than 8 cm and less than 12 cm. I can calculate the arithmetic mean of my two estimates."
She records:

$8 + 12 = 20 \xrightarrow{\text{can be written as}} \triangle + \triangle = 20 \longrightarrow 2(\triangle) = 20 \longrightarrow 2(10) = 20$

$10 + 10 = 20$, so the arithmetic mean of 8 and 12 is 10.

She says: "I think that a fairly accurate estimate of the length of my pencil is 10 cm and it will probably not be in error by more than 2 cm."

To find a fairly accurate measurement of the length of her pencil, Mary uses a rule marked in millimetres.

> 10 millimetres have the same length as 1 cm.
> We write millimetre as mm.
> 1 millimetre has the same length as 0·1 cm.

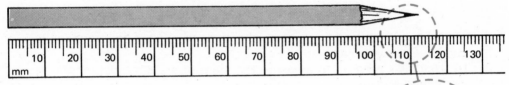

Mary measures the length of the pencil twice and records her results in this way.

		1st	2nd
Length of pencil	cm and mm	11 cm 1 mm	11 cm 3 mm
	decimal form	11·1 cm	11·3 cm

She calculates that the mean length is 11·2 cm.

She says: "I think that a fairly accurate measurement of the length of my pencil is 11·2 cm, and it will probably not be in error by more than 0·1 cm."

1 Use Mary's method and calculate a fairly accurate measurement of the length of:

a] a hand span.

b] a foot length.

c] a stride.

d] a curved line segment.

e] a ribbon.

f] a toy car.

g] a piece of string.

h] a middle finger length.

i] a crayon.

j] an arm length.

MEASURING MASS ACCURATELY

Jill and Liz are discussing ways of measuring the mass of 1 cube as accurately as they can. They have 10 g, 20 g, 50 g, and 100 g masses and a balance to help them.

Liz measures the mass of 10 cubes. She records:

10 cubes $\xrightarrow{\text{have a total mass less than}}$ 60 g, so 1 cube $\longrightarrow \frac{60}{10}$ g or 6 g.

10 cubes $\xrightarrow{\text{have a total mass greater than}}$ 50 g so 1 cube $\longrightarrow \frac{50}{10}$ g or 5 g.

Liz says: "I cannot be certain what the accurate measurement of the mass of 1 cube is. I think it must be greater than 5 g and less than 6 g."

Jill uses the 20 g mass to measure. She records:

3 cubes $\xrightarrow{\text{have a total mass less than}}$ 20 g, so 1 cube $\longrightarrow \frac{20}{3}$ g or $6\frac{2}{3}$ g.

4 cubes $\xrightarrow{\text{have a total mass greater than}}$ 20 g, so 1 cube $\longrightarrow \frac{20}{4}$ g or 5 g.

Jill says: "I think the accurate measurement of the mass of 1 cube is between 5 g and $6\frac{2}{3}$ g."

1 a] Use Liz's method to measure the mass of a 2 centimetre cube as accurately as you can.
b] Use Jill's method to measure the mass of a 2 centimetre cube as accurately as you can.

2 Do you think that all your cubes have exactly the same mass?

3 a] Repeat Exercise 1 a] using 20 cubes instead of 10 cubes.
b] Repeat Exercise 1 b] using a 40 g mass instead of a 20 g mass.

4 Using a spring balance, find as accurately as you can the mass of a cube. Do you think this result is more or less accurate than your other results?

5 Repeat Exercises 1 and 3 using marbles instead of cubes.

6 Using any method you wish, measure the mass of a drawing pin as accurately as you can.

7 Complete the matrix.

Number of objects	10	20	25	40	30	50	60	35	45
Total mass is greater than (g)	60	80	180	90	180	300	300	70	90
Total mass is less than (g)	70	90	200	100	200	320	320	80	100
One object has a mass between □ g and △ g	6 g and 7 g								

MEASURING ANGLES ACCURATELY

Margaret measures as accurately as she can the angles of this triangle.

She records: ∠A measures approximately 63°.
∠B measures approximately 70°.
∠C measures approximately 46°.

63 + 70 + 46 = 179

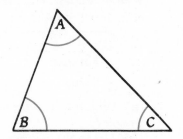

Margaret says: "I know that the total angular measurement of the angles of a triangle is 180°. The total error in my measurement is 1°. I cannot be certain what the accurate measurement of each angle is but I think that each of my measurements will not be in error by more than 1 or 2 degrees."

1 a] Measure as accurately as you can each of the angles of these triangles.
b] For each triangle, calculate the sum of your results and record your total error.

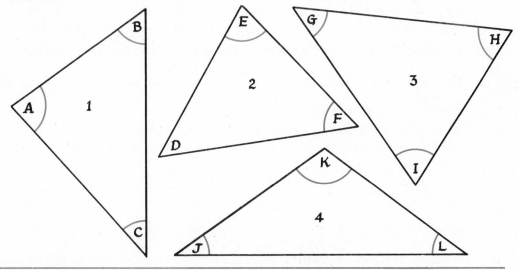

2 Complete the matrix about the measurements of the angles of these triangles.

Measurement of 1st angle	89°	57°	72°			119°	65°	115°
Measurement of 2nd angle	58°	62°	53°	40°	46°	29°	104°	23°
Measurement of 3rd angle	31°	60°	57°	39°	48°	30°	13°	
Total angular measurement				178°	181°			179°
Total error								

31

ENRICHMENT

1 Fergus and Stan each measure the length of the school corridor with a trundle wheel. They then each check their measurement, first using a metre rule and secondly a tape. They record their results.

	Trundle wheel	Metre rule	Tape
Fergus	$18\frac{1}{2}$ m	18·61 m	18·74 m
Stan	$18\frac{3}{4}$ m	18·80 m	18·70 m

a] Which of the three methods do you think will give the most accurate result?

b] Using the six measurements, calculate the median length.

2 Complete the sentences.

a] I think that a fairly accurate estimate of the length of the corridor is ☐ m.

b] The measurement will probably not be in error by more than △ m.

3 Joy, Beth, and Janet each measure the width of a small book with a 20 cm rule and with a tape. They record their results.

	Joy	Beth	Janet
20 cm rule	8·0 cm	8·3 cm	8·4 cm
Tape	8·2 cm	8·5 cm	8·2 cm

a] What is the difference between the greatest and the least of these measurements?

b] Calculate the mean of Joy's results. Repeat for Beth's and Janet's results.

4 Complete the sentences.

a] I think that a fairly accurate estimate of the width of the book is ☐ cm.

b] The measurement will probably not be in error by more than △ cm.

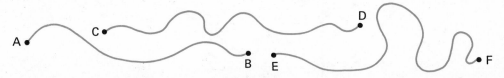

5 Measure twice in millimetres, as accurately as you can, the length of each of these curved line segments. Record your results, then complete the matrix.

	1st (mm)	2nd (mm)	Mean (mm)	Fairly accurate measurement (mm)	Possible error (mm)
$\overline{AB}$					
$\overline{CD}$					
$\overline{EF}$					

6 Complete the sentence.

I think the total length of the three curved line segments is greater than ☐ mm and less than △ mm.

32

Section 6 · Algebraic Relations

PATTERNS ON A LATTICE

1 Make two sets of plasticine balls each with masses of 1 unit, 2 units, 3 units, 4 units, 5 units, and 6 units. Use different coloured plasticine for each set. Also make one extra 6 unit plasticine ball in another colour.

1st set: □{1, 2, 3, 4, 5, 6}   2nd set: △{1, 2, 3, 4, 5, 6}

2 a] Taking one mass from each set, find as many different pairs of masses as you can to balance a 6 unit mass.

b] Record your numbers as ordered pairs in a matrix.

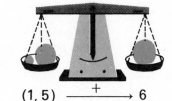

□	1				
△	5				

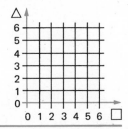

$(1, 5) \xrightarrow{+} 6$

3 a] Draw a 6 × 6 lattice on squared paper. Mark each ordered pair from your matrix as a black point on it.
b] What do you notice about the position of the points?
c] Have you found all the ordered pairs?
d] Does each ordered pair make □ + △ = 6 true?

4 a] Repeat Exercise 2. This time find as many different pairs of masses as you can which together are lighter than the 6 unit mass.
b] Mark each ordered pair as a green point on the 6 × 6 lattice.
c] What do you notice about the position of the points?
d] Have you found all the ordered pairs?
e] Does each ordered pair make □ + △ < 6 true?

5 a] Repeat Exercise 2. This time find as many different pairs of masses as you can which together are heavier than the 6 unit mass.
b] Mark each ordered pair as a red point on the 6 × 6 lattice.
c] What do you notice about the position of the points?
d] Have you found all the ordered pairs?
e] Does each ordered pair make □ + △ > 6 true?

6 Write about the pattern of points on your 6 × 6 lattice.

PATTERNS ON A LATTICE

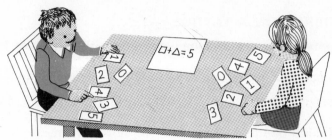

Linda and Eric each have a set of cards. The cards are numbered 0, 1, 2, 3, 4, and 5.

Linda's: □{0, 1, 2, 3, 4, 5}　Eric's: △{0, 1, 2, 3, 4, 5}

1　They want to find all the ordered pairs that will make □ + △ = 5 true.

a] Write down all the ordered pairs that Linda and Eric can find.
b] Draw a 5 × 5 lattice on squared paper. Mark each ordered pair as a black point on it.

We say you have graphed the ordered pairs.

2　Linda and Eric now find an ordered pair, (4, 0), whose sum is less than 5.

a] Write down all the ordered pairs that will make □ + △ < 5 true.
b] Graph each ordered pair as a green point on the 5 × 5 lattice.

3　Linda and Eric now find an ordered pair (5, 1) whose sum is greater than 5.

a] Write down all the ordered pairs that will make □ + △ > 5 true.
b] Graph each ordered pair as a red point on the 5 × 5 lattice.

4　Are there any points on the lattice left unmarked?

5　Write about the pattern of points on the 5 × 5 lattice.

6　Make two sets of cards numbered from 0 to 10. Using a 10 × 10 lattice, graph all the ordered pairs that will make:

□ + △ = 10 true as black points,
□ + △ < 10 true as green points,
□ + △ > 10 true as red points.

7　Write about the pattern of points on the 10 × 10 lattice.

8　Play the Sum Game.

34

COLLINEAR POINTS

Brenda and John are playing the Greater Than and Less Than Game.
Each throws a pair of dice in turn. One die is white and the other is blue.

Brenda scores if she throws a
pair with a total less than 7,

$\square + \triangle < 7$.

John scores if he throws a
pair with a total greater than 7,

$\square + \triangle > 7$.

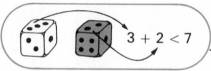

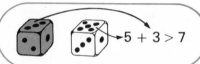

They graph their scoring pairs as points on
a 6 × 6 lattice. Brenda graphs her points
in blue. John graphs his points in black.
If a pair totals 7, the point is not graphed
on the lattice and there is no score.

After each has had 10 throws, Brenda has two
more points on the lattice, and wins the game.

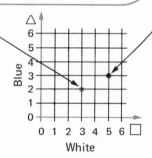

1   Play the Greater Than and Less Than Game with a friend.

2   a] Draw a 7 × 7 lattice on squared paper.
     b] Write down all the ordered pairs that will make $\square + \triangle = 7$ true.
     c] Graph each ordered pair as a green point on the lattice.
     d] What do you notice about your set of green points?

Your set of green points all lie in a straight line. We say they are collinear.

3   a] Draw an 8 × 8 lattice on squared paper.
     b] Write down all the ordered pairs that will make $\square + \triangle = 8$ true.
     c] Graph each ordered pair as a blue point on the lattice.
     d] Are your points collinear?

4   Play the Odds or Evens Game.

COLLINEAR POINTS

Using these two sets, Sally and Frank find all the ordered pairs that will make $\square + \triangle = 1$ true.

$\square\{0, \frac{1}{2}, 1\}$ $\triangle\{0, \frac{1}{2}, 1\}$

They record the ordered pairs in a matrix.

$\square$	$\triangle$
0	1
$\frac{1}{2}$	$\frac{1}{2}$
1	0

They then graph the ordered pairs.

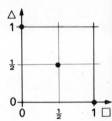

1 **a]** Using these two sets, find all the ordered pairs that will make $\square + \triangle = 1$ true.

$\square\{0, \frac{1}{4}, \frac{1}{2}, \frac{3}{4}, 1\}$ $\triangle\{0, \frac{1}{4}, \frac{1}{2}, \frac{3}{4}, 1\}$

b] Record the ordered pairs in a matrix.

$\square$	$\triangle$
0	1

c] Draw this lattice on squared paper. Graph all your ordered pairs.

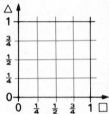

2 **a]** Using these two sets, find all the ordered pairs that will make $\square + \triangle = 1$ true.

$\square\{0, \frac{1}{8}, \frac{1}{4}, \frac{3}{8}, \frac{1}{2}, \frac{5}{8}, \frac{3}{4}, \frac{7}{8}, 1\}$ $\triangle\{0, \frac{1}{8}, \frac{1}{4}, \frac{3}{8}, \frac{1}{2}, \frac{3}{4}, \frac{7}{8}, 1\}$

b] Record the ordered pairs in a matrix.

$\square$	$\triangle$
0	1
$\frac{1}{8}$	$\frac{7}{8}$

c] Draw this lattice on squared paper. Graph all your ordered pairs.

Joan uses each pair of sets to find the ordered pairs that will make $\square + \triangle = 1$ true. She graphs her ordered pairs.

$\square\{0, \frac{1}{10}, \frac{1}{5}, \frac{3}{10} \cdots 1\}$
$\triangle\{0, \frac{1}{10}, \frac{1}{5}, \frac{3}{10} \cdots 1\}$

$\square\{0, \frac{1}{20}, \frac{1}{10}, \frac{3}{20} \cdots 1\}$
$\triangle\{0, \frac{1}{20}, \frac{1}{10}, \frac{3}{20} \cdots 1\}$

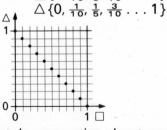

3 What do you notice about each graph?

4 Play the Midpoint Game.

36

LINE GRAPHS

1
a] Draw this lattice on squared paper.
b] Do each of these ordered pairs make
□ + △ = 2 true?

(0, 2) $(\frac{1}{2}, 1\frac{1}{2})$ $(1\frac{1}{4}, \frac{3}{4})$ $(1\frac{1}{2}, \frac{1}{2})$ $(\frac{1}{4}, 1\frac{3}{4})$

c] Graph each ordered pair as a black point.
d] What do you notice?

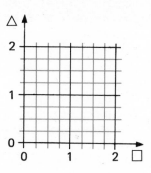

2
a] Write down some more ordered pairs that will make □ + △ = 2 true.
b] Graph each ordered pair as a red point.
c] Do these red points lie on the same straight line as the black points?

3
a] Join all the points you have graphed by drawing a straight line.
b] How many points lie on this line?
c] Could you name them all?

We say the graph of □ + △ = 2 is a straight line graph.

4
a] Draw this lattice on squared paper.
b] Complete the ordered pairs that will make □ + △ = 3 true.

(0, △)   (1, △)   (2, △)   (3, △)

c] Graph each ordered pair.
d] Draw the straight line graph □ + △ = 3.
e] Write down the addresses of some more points on the line.
f] Do each of these ordered pairs make □ + △ = 3 true?

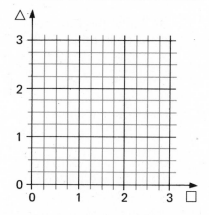

5 Repeat Exercise 4 graphing the ordered pairs that will:

a] make □ + △ = 4 true using a 4 × 4 lattice.
b] make □ + △ = 5 true using a 5 × 5 lattice.

6 Draw the graph of □ + △ = 9.

Section 7 · Sorting and Classifying Shapes

FORMING A PARALLELOGRAM AND A RHOMBUS

You will need a wide ruler and a narrower ruler.

1

a] Holding the wide ruler firmly on a piece of paper, draw a line segment along each of the longer edges.

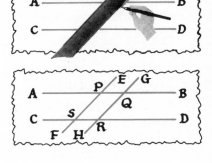

b] Label these line segments, AB and CD. $\overline{AB}$ and $\overline{CD}$ have the same direction.
We say line segments which have the same direction are parallel.

c] Hold the narrower ruler so that the edges cross $\overline{AB}$ and $\overline{CD}$. Draw a line segment along each of the longer edges.

d] Label these line segments, EF and GH.

e] Label the four points where the lines cross each other P, Q, R, and S.
You have now formed a shape we call a parallelogram.

2 Measure in millimetres the lengths of the four sides of the parallelogram, $\overline{PQ}$, $\overline{SR}$, $\overline{QR}$, and $\overline{PS}$. What do you notice?

3 Use the two rulers to form a different parallelogram. Repeat Exercise 2. What do you notice?

4 Use the wide ruler twice to form a parallelogram. Label the vertices W, X, Y, and Z. You have formed a special parallelogram we call a rhombus. Repeat Exercise 2. What do you notice?

5 Investigate your parallelogram PQRS and your rhombus WXYZ for axes of line symmetry. Use a mirror to help if you wish. Write about your discoveries.

6 Cut out your parallelogram and your rhombus. Investigate each shape for rotational symmetry. Write about your discoveries.

FORMING A RECTANGLE AND A SQUARE

You will need a protractor or a set square, a wide ruler, and a narrower ruler.

1 **a]** Use the wide ruler to draw two parallel line segments, $\overline{AB}$ and $\overline{CD}$. Mark a point W on $\overline{AB}$. Use the protractor or set square to form the right angle, AWX.

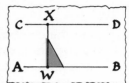

Because ∠AWX is a right angle, we say $\overline{WX}$ is perpendicular to $\overline{AB}$ and $\overline{AB}$ is perpendicular to $\overline{WX}$.

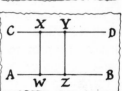

b] Use the narrower ruler to form a parallelogram, WXYZ. You have formed a special parallelogram we call a rectangle.

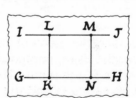

2 Complete the sentences.

a] ∠WXY measures approximately □°.
b] ∠XYZ measures approximately □°.
c] ∠YZW measures approximately □°.
d] ∠ZWX measures approximately □°.

e] $\overline{YZ}$ is perpendicular to __.
f] $\overline{YZ}$ is also perpendicular to __.

3 Use the wide ruler twice and the protractor or set square to form a different rectangle, KLMN. You have formed a special rectangle and a special rhombus we call a square.

4 Investigate rectangle WXYZ and square KLMN for axes of line symmetry. Write about your discoveries.

5 Cut out your rectangle and your square. Investigate each shape for rotational symmetry. Write about your discoveries.

6 **a]** Use the protractor and both rulers to draw this rectangle pattern. How many rectangles are there?
b] Draw a fourth line segment parallel to $\overline{XY}$. How many rectangles are there now?
c] Continue the pattern.

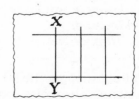

FORMING AN EQUILATERAL TRIANGLE AND AN ISOSCELES TRIANGLE

You will need a pair of compasses, a ruler, a protractor, scissors, and cardboard.

1 On the cardboard draw $\overline{AB}$ 8 cm in length. Using compasses, draw one arc with centre A and radius 8 cm. Draw another arc with centre B and the same radius. Label the point of intersection X. Draw $\overline{AX}$ and $\overline{BX}$.

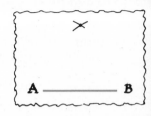

You have formed a special triangle we call an equilateral triangle.

2 a] Measure and record the length of each side of triangle AXB.
b] Using a protractor, measure and record the size of each angle of the triangle.
c] What do you think the exact measurement of each angle should be?

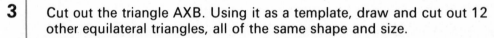

3 Cut out the triangle AXB. Using it as a template, draw and cut out 12 other equilateral triangles, all of the same shape and size.

We say the 13 triangles are congruent.

4 Fit your equilateral triangles together without leaving any spaces.

You have formed a tessellation. We say equilateral triangles tessellate.

5 On another piece of cardboard draw $\overline{PQ}$ 8 cm in length. Using compasses, draw one arc with centre P and radius 10 cm. Draw another arc with centre Q and the same radius. Label the point of intersection X. Draw $\overline{PX}$ and $\overline{QX}$.

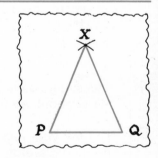

You have formed a special triangle we call an isosceles triangle.

6 a] Measure and record the length of each side of triangle PXQ.
b] Using a protractor, measure and record the size of each angle of the triangle.
c] What do you notice about the triangle?

7 Cut out triangle PXQ. Using it as a template, draw and cut out 12 other congruent isosceles triangles. Do the isosceles triangles tessellate?

ASSIGNMENT: TESSELLATION SHEET

You will need coloured
pencils and a tessellation
sheet like this.

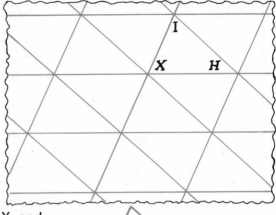

1 Outline with a coloured
pencil any plane shapes you
can find on the sheet. Record
the names of each different
shape.

2 Label the angles of one triangle, I, X, and
H as shown. Cut out the triangle.

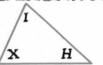

3 Use your labelled triangle to mark on the tessellation sheet other angles
with the same angular measurement as: **a]** ∠X. **b]** ∠I. **c]** ∠H.

4 What is the total angular measurement of: **a]** a complete turn?
b] half a complete turn?

5 Using an intersection with these angles marked on it, find the total
angular measurement of:

a] H° + I° + X° + H° + I° + X°.
b] H° + I° + X°.
c] the angles of any triangle on
your tessellation sheet.

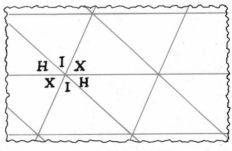

6 **a]** Outline a parallelogram like this.
Then label the angles as they are
marked on your tessellation sheet.
b] What is the sum of the angular
measurements of the angles of
the parallelogram,
H° + X° + I° + □° + △° + ▨°?
c] What do you notice about the
opposite angles of the parallelogram?

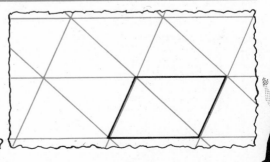

ENRICHMENT: PROPERTIES OF PLANE SHAPES

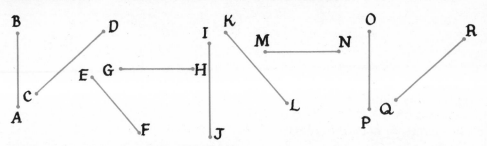

1 Look at the set of line segments. Continue and complete the matrix.

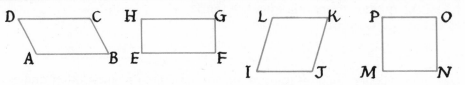

Line segments parallel to each other	Line segments perpendicular to each other
$\overline{AB}$ and $\overline{JI}$	

2 Look at the set of plane shapes. Which of these sentences are true?

a] ABCD is a parallelogram.   b] EFGH is a parallelogram.
c] IJKL is a parallelogram.   d] MNOP is a parallelogram.
e] ABCD is a rectangle.   f] EFGH is a rectangle.
g] IJKL is a rectangle.   h] MNOP is a rectangle.
i] ABCD is a rhombus.   j] EFGH is a rhombus.
k] IJKL is a rhombus.   l] MNOP is a rhombus.
m] ABCD is a square.   n] EFGH is a square.
o] IJKL is a square.   p] MNOP is a square.

3 Draw arrows to complete the relations.

a]

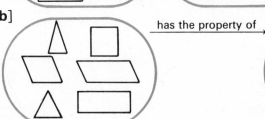

is called →

has the property of →

a parallelogram
a rhombus
a rectangle
a square

opposite sides equal
all sides equal
opposite angles equal
all angles right angles

b]

has the property of →

no axis of symmetry
exactly one axis of symmetry
exactly two axes of symmetry
exactly three axes of symmetry
exactly four axes of symmetry
rotational symmetry

ENRICHMENT: FORMING POLYOMINOES

You will need 2 cm squared paper, a mirror, and coloured pencils.

We call this shape a domino. It is formed by fitting two squares together so that they have a common side.

This shape is not a domino.
The two squares forming the shape only have a common vertex.

We call these shapes trominoes.
They are formed by fitting three squares together so that each square has at least one side in common with another square.

Tromino A   Tromino B

1 From the squared paper, cut out three squares each with sides of 2 cm. How many different trominoes can you form by arranging your three squares?

2 On the squared paper, colour in two trominoes like B and C.

a] Cut out the trominoes. Are they congruent?
b] Are trominoes A and B congruent?
c] Why do you think we say there are only two different trominoes?

3 Investigate trominoes A and B for line and rotational symmetry. Record your discoveries.

4 a] Will tromino B tessellate? If it does, colour in a tessellation on squared paper.
b] Can you find a different tessellation? If so, colour this in.

We call these shapes tetrominoes.
They are formed by fitting four squares together so that each square has at least one side in common with another square.

5 Colour in as many different tetrominoes as you can on squared paper.

a] Investigate each tetromino for line and rotational symmetry.
b] Which of your tetrominoes tessellate? Colour in your tessellations on squared paper.
c] Which of your tetrominoes has the least perimeter and which has the greatest perimeter?
d] What can you say about the area measurement of each tetromino?

6 Play the Pentomino Game.

43

Section 8 · Multiplication

DISTRIBUTING OVER ADDITION

The pleasure steamer can carry a maximum of 72 passengers on each trip. She makes 24 trips each week. What is the maximum number of passengers she could carry in a week?

The children use different methods to find the maximum number of passengers.

Don 72 × 24 —can be written as→ (70 + 2) × (20 + 4)
(70 × 20) + (70 × 4) + (2 × 20) + (2 × 4)
(1400 + 280 + 40 + 8) ————————→1728

Judy 72 × 24 ————→72 × (20 + 4)
(72 × 20) + (72 × 4)
(1440 + 288) ————————→1728

Sam 72 × 24 ————→(70 + 2) × 24
(70 × 24) + (2 × 24)
(1680 + 48) ————————→1728

The maximum number of passengers is 1728.

1 Use one of the children's methods to complete the matrix.

Maximum number of passengers each trip	56	38	45	27	35	38	41	45	34
Number of trips	25	32	34	26	18	24	28	32	24
Maximum number of passengers	1400								

2 The pleasure steamer carried 1728 passengers one week with a maximum of 72 passengers on each trip. Find the least number of trips she needed to make.

3 Find the products.

a] 34
×24

b] 42
×36

c] 56
×20

d] 60
×32

e] 48
×23

f] 37
×31

g] 45
×27

44

FINDING PRODUCTS

The ferry boat can carry a maximum of 48 cars. If she makes 29 trips, what is the maximum number of cars she could carry?

Jill and Brian use different methods to find the maximum number of cars.

Jill   48
       × 29
        72 (8 × 9)
     360 (40 × 9)
     160 (8 × 20)
     800 (40 × 20)
   1392 (48 × 29)

Brian   48
        × 29
       432 (48 × 9)
      960 (48 × 20)
   1392 (48 × 29)

The maximum number of cars is 1392.

1   Use Jill's method to complete the matrix.

Maximum number of cars each trip	32	36	37	39	24	30	36	48	39	43
Number of trips	52	55	63	54	24	36	40	48	27	28
Maximum number of cars	1664									

2   Use any method to complete the matrix.

Maximum number of cars each trip	54	63	29	34	50	61	73	35	46	55
Number of trips	17	39	47	28	30	23	62	19	29	24
Maximum number of cars										

3   Find the products.

a] 28 × 22   b] 35 × 27   c] 34 × 23   d] 34 × 24   e] 27 × 22
f] 25 × 35   g] 27 × 35   h] 27 × 45   i] 28 × 45   j] 48 × 70
k] 48 × 72   l] 24 × 72   m] 24 × 36   n] 24 × 18   o] 48 × 18
p] 63 × 32   q] 64 × 32   r] 64 × 33   s] 72 × 21   t] 75 × 25

FINDING PRODUCTS

A jet can carry a maximum of 125 passengers on each flight. What is the maximum number of passengers it can carry on 7 flights?
The children use different methods to find the maximum number of passengers.

Paul 125×7 —can be written as→ $(100 + 20 + 5) \times 7$
$(100 \times 7) + (20 \times 7) + (5 \times 7)$
$(700 + 140 + 35)$ ————→ 875

Liz

H	T	U
1	2	5
7	14	35
7	17	5
8	7	5

$\Big\} \times 7$

Joy
```
    125
  ×   7
  ─────
     35   (5 × 7)
    140   (20 × 7)
    700   (100 × 7)
  ─────
    875   (125 × 7)
```

The maximum number of passengers is 875.

1 Find the products using one of the children's methods.

a] 248×6 b] 272×7 c] 329×5 d] 459×9 e] 572×4
f] 698×8 g] 783×3 h] 207×7 i] 230×2 j] 320×6

Another jet can carry a maximum of 125 passengers on each flight. What is the maximum number of passengers it can carry on 27 flights?
Colin finds the maximum number using this method.

125×27 —can be written as→ $(100 + 20 + 5) \times (20 + 7)$
$(100 \times 20) + (20 \times 20) + (5 \times 20)$
$+ (100 \times 7) + (20 \times 7) + (5 \times 7)$
$(2000 + 400 + 100 + 700 + 140 + 35)$ ——→ 3375

The maximum number of passengers is 3375.

2 Use Colin's method to complete the matrix.

Maximum number of passengers each flight	134	118	123	142	156	104	131	108
Number of flights	25	24	26	32	31	26	53	49
Maximum number of passengers								

FINDING PRODUCTS

The chocolate machine, which holds 148 bars of chocolate, was completely refilled 28 times during one month. When the machine was empty for the twenty-eighth time, how many bars had been sold?

Sara and Dennis use different methods to find the total number of bars sold.

Sara   148
    × 28
      64   (8 × 8)
   320 (40 × 8)
   800 (100 × 8)
   160   (8 × 20)
   800 (40 × 20)
 2000 (100 × 20)
 4144 (148 × 28)

Dennis   148
    × 28
 1184 (148 × 8)
 2960 (148 × 20)
 4144 (148 × 28)

The total number of bars is 4144.

Use any method to complete each matrix.

1

Number of bars machine holds	165	144	224	150	214	149	162	127	204
Number of times completely refilled	31	29	28	30	23	17	25	19	20
Total number of bars sold	5115								

2

Number of stamps machine holds	275	336	412	500	288	336	144	250	256
Number of times completely refilled	36	45	27	24	25	42	50	17	34
Total number of stamps sold									

Use any method to find the products.

3   a] 461 × 37   b] 164 × 73   c] 614 × 27   d] 641 × 72   e] 879 × 36

4   a]   256   b]   266   c]   366   d]   366   e]   366   f]   423   g]   372
       × 23   × 23   × 23   × 24   × 34   × 26   × 42

5

a] 8288 stamps are sold from a machine during one month. The machine is completely refilled 28 times. How many stamps does the machine hold when it is full?

b] 2072 bars of chocolate are sold from a machine during one month. The machine is completely refilled with 148 bars each time. How many times is the machine filled?

MULTIPLICATION SITUATIONS

23 members of Class 6 are visiting the airport. The rail fare is £2·25 each return. What is the total rail fare?

The children find the total rail fare using different methods.

Tony writes: £2·25 × 23———→225p × 23
Gwen writes: £2·25 × 23———→(£2·00 + 20p + 5p) × 23
                       ———→(£2·00 + 20p + 5p) × (20 + 3)

```
Tony   225
      × 23
       15    (5 ×  3)
       60    (20 × 3)
      600   (200 × 3)
      100   (5 × 20)
      400   (20 × 20)
     4000  (200 × 20)
     5175  (225 × 23)
      225p × 23 = 5175p =  £51·75
```

```
Gwen   (£2·00 +  20p +   5p)
     ×               20
     (£40·00 + 400p + 100p)
     (£40·00 + £4·00 + £1·00) = £45·00

   + (£2·00 +  20p +   5p)
     ×                 3
     (£6·00 +  60p +  15p)  = £6·75

     £45·00 + £6·75          = £51·75
```

Rose writes: £2·25 × 23———→(£2·00 + 20p + 5p) × 23

```
Rose     (£2·00 + 20p + 5p)
     ×                   23
     (£46·00 + 460p + 115p)———→(£46·00 + £4·60 + £1·15)———→ £51·75
```

The total rail fare was £51·75.

Use any method to complete each matrix.

1

Cost of each fare	£3·15	£2·60	£3·45	£1·87	£2·36	£3·79	£2·81	£1·93
Number travelling	27	35	24	38	30	28	34	17
Total rail fare	£85·05							

2

Cost of each fare	£4·25	£3·63	£3·40	£2·05	£3·18	£2·45	£1·72	£3·65
Number travelling	15	26	29	32	24	23	18	27
Total rail fare								

MULTIPLICATION: QUICK METHODS

The children are discussing quick methods of finding products. They each use a different method to find the product of 18×35.

Lucy writes:

$18 \times 35 = 18 \times (5 \times 7) = (18 \times 5) \times 7 = 90 \times 7 = 630$

David writes:

$18 \times 35 = (2 \times 9) \times (5 \times 7) = (2 \times 5) \times (9 \times 7) = 10 \times 63 = 630$

Ivor writes:

$18 \times 35 = (20 - 2) \times 35 = (20 \times 35) - (2 \times 35) = 700 - 70 = 630$

The product of 18×35 is 630.

1   Use any quick method to find the products.

a] 19×23 b] 14×25 c] 28×24 d] 77×12 e] 16×35
f] 18×45 g] 49×17 h] 46×16 i] 23×18 j] 27×16
k] 14×55 l] 98×33 m] 34×14 n] 24×15 o] 99×46
p] 29×23 q] 14×65 r] 25×25 s] 33×18 t] 49×24

Leslie knows that $18 \times 35 = 630$.

She says: "If I halve 18 and double 35, the product will also be 630 because $18 \times 35 = (9 \times 2) \times 35 = 9 \times (2 \times 35) = 9 \times 70$."

2   Use $64 \times 24 = 1536$ to help you find the products.

a] 32×48 b] 16×96 c] 128×12 d] 32×24 e] 32×12
f] 16×48 g] 128×24 h] 64×48 i] 8×192 j] 256×6

3   Use $56 \times 48 = 2688$ to help you find the products.

a] 28×48 b] 14×48 c] 56×24 d] 56×12 e] 112×48

4   Write down any other products you can find quickly using $56 \times 48 = 2688$.

5   Use $15 \times 60 = 900$ to help you find the products.

a] 15×30 b] 30×60 c] 45×20 d] 90×40 e] 15×120

6   Write down any other products you can find quickly using $15 \times 60 = 900$.

7   For each of these, use five different methods to find the products.

a] 25×28 b] 32×19 c] 36×15

8   Play the Speedy Product Game.

Section 9 · Fractions

MULTIPLICATION OF FRACTIONS

Each disc in the set of discs has been cut in half.

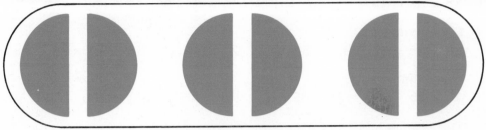

$\frac{1}{2} + \frac{1}{2} + \frac{1}{2} + \frac{1}{2} + \frac{1}{2} + \frac{1}{2}$ $\xrightarrow{\text{can be written as}}$ $6\left(\frac{1}{2}\right) \longrightarrow \frac{1}{2} \times 6 \longrightarrow 3$

We say the product of $\frac{1}{2}$ and 6 is equivalent to the product of 6 and $\frac{1}{2}$. The product is 3.

1 Draw pictures of discs to help you find the products.

a] $\frac{1}{3} + \frac{1}{3} + \frac{1}{3} + \frac{1}{3} + \frac{1}{3} + \frac{1}{3} \longrightarrow \triangle\left(\frac{1}{3}\right) \longrightarrow \frac{1}{3} \times \triangle \longrightarrow \square$
The product of $\frac{1}{3}$ and $\triangle$ also $\triangle$ and $\frac{1}{3}$ is $\square$.

b] $\frac{1}{4} + \frac{1}{4} + \frac{1}{4} + \frac{1}{4} + \frac{1}{4} + \frac{1}{4} + \frac{1}{4} + \frac{1}{4} \longrightarrow \triangle\left(\frac{1}{4}\right) \longrightarrow \frac{1}{4} \times \triangle \longrightarrow \square$
The product of $\frac{1}{4}$ and $\triangle$ also $\triangle$ and $\frac{1}{4}$ is $\square$.

c] $\frac{1}{5} + \frac{1}{5} + \frac{1}{5} + \frac{1}{5} + \frac{1}{5} + \frac{1}{5} + \frac{1}{5} + \frac{1}{5} + \frac{1}{5} + \frac{1}{5} \longrightarrow \triangle\left(\frac{1}{5}\right) \longrightarrow \frac{1}{5} \times \triangle \longrightarrow \square$
The product of $\frac{1}{5}$ and $\triangle$ also $\triangle$ and $\frac{1}{5}$ is $\square$.

d] $\frac{1}{2} + \frac{1}{2} + \frac{1}{2} + \frac{1}{2} + \frac{1}{2} + \frac{1}{2} + \frac{1}{2} + \frac{1}{2} \longrightarrow \triangle\left(\frac{1}{2}\right) \longrightarrow \frac{1}{2} \times \triangle \longrightarrow \square$
The product of $\frac{1}{2}$ and $\triangle$ also $\triangle$ and $\frac{1}{2}$ is $\square$.

There are 6 boys in the set.
Half of the boys have a dog.
Three boys have a dog.

$\frac{1}{2}$ of 6 $\xrightarrow{\text{can be written as}}$ 3

2 Draw pictures to help you complete the sentences.

a] There are 6 girls in the set.
One third of the girls have a hat.
$\square$ of the girls have a hat.
$\frac{1}{3}$ of 6 $\longrightarrow \square$

b] There are 8 animals in the set.
One fourth of the animals are cats.
$\square$ of the animals are cats.
$\frac{1}{4}$ of 8 $\longrightarrow \square$

c] There are 10 men in the set.
One fifth of the men wear glasses.
$\square$ of the men wear glasses.
$\triangle$ of 10 $\longrightarrow \square$

d] There are 8 shapes in the set.
One half of the shapes are squares.
$\square$ of the shapes are squares.
$\triangle$ of 8 $\longrightarrow \square$

MULTIPLICATION OF FRACTIONS

Angus has $3\frac{1}{2}$ bars of chocolate.
He breaks the 3 bars into halves.
He now has 7 half bars.

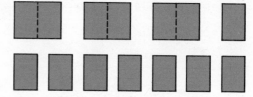

He records: $3\frac{1}{2} \xrightarrow{\text{can be written as}} 7$ halves $\longrightarrow 7(\frac{1}{2}) \longrightarrow \frac{1}{2} \times 7 \longrightarrow \frac{7}{2}$

1 Complete. Draw pictures to help if you wish.

a] $4\frac{1}{2} \longrightarrow \square$ halves $\longrightarrow \square(\frac{1}{2}) \longrightarrow \frac{\square}{2}$

b] $2\frac{3}{8} \longrightarrow \square$ eighths $\longrightarrow \square(\frac{1}{\triangle}) \longrightarrow \frac{\square}{\triangle}$

c] $1\frac{1}{4} \longrightarrow \square$ fourths $\longrightarrow \square(\frac{1}{\triangle}) \longrightarrow \frac{\square}{\triangle}$

d] $3\frac{1}{3} \longrightarrow \square$ thirds $\longrightarrow \square(\frac{1}{3}) \longrightarrow \frac{\square}{3}$

e] $4\frac{1}{5} \longrightarrow \square$ fifths $\longrightarrow \square(\frac{1}{\triangle}) \longrightarrow \frac{\square}{\triangle}$

f] $6\frac{5}{6} \longrightarrow \square$ sixths $\longrightarrow \square(\frac{1}{\triangle}) \longrightarrow \frac{\square}{\triangle}$

$\frac{1}{6} + \frac{1}{6} + \frac{1}{6} + \frac{1}{6} + \frac{1}{6} \xrightarrow{\text{can be written as}} 5(\frac{1}{6}) \longrightarrow \frac{1}{6} \times 5 \longrightarrow \frac{5}{6}$

2 Complete.

a] $\frac{1}{5} + \frac{1}{5} + \frac{1}{5} + \frac{1}{5} \longrightarrow \square(\frac{1}{5}) \longrightarrow \frac{1}{5} \times \square \longrightarrow \frac{\square}{5}$

b] $\frac{1}{3} + \frac{1}{3} \longrightarrow \square(\frac{1}{3}) \longrightarrow \frac{1}{3} \times \square \longrightarrow \frac{\square}{3}$

c] $\frac{1}{4} + \frac{1}{4} + \frac{1}{4} \longrightarrow \square(\frac{1}{4}) \longrightarrow \frac{1}{4} \times \square \longrightarrow \frac{\square}{4}$

d] $\frac{1}{8} + \frac{1}{8} + \frac{1}{8} + \frac{1}{8} + \frac{1}{8} \longrightarrow \square(\frac{1}{8}) \longrightarrow \frac{1}{8} \times \square \longrightarrow \frac{\square}{8}$

$\frac{3}{5} + \frac{3}{5} + \frac{3}{5} + \frac{3}{5} \xrightarrow{\text{can be written as}} 4(\frac{3}{5}) \longrightarrow \frac{3}{5} \times 4 \longrightarrow \frac{12}{5} \longrightarrow 2\frac{2}{5}$

3 Complete.

a] $\frac{2}{3} + \frac{2}{3} \longrightarrow \square(\frac{2}{3}) \longrightarrow \frac{2}{3} \times \square \longrightarrow \frac{\triangle}{3} \longrightarrow \boxed{}$

b] $\frac{3}{4} + \frac{3}{4} + \frac{3}{4} \longrightarrow \square(\frac{3}{4}) \longrightarrow \frac{3}{4} \times \square \longrightarrow \frac{\triangle}{4} \longrightarrow \boxed{}$

c] $\frac{5}{8} + \frac{5}{8} + \frac{5}{8} + \frac{5}{8} + \frac{5}{8} \longrightarrow \square(\frac{5}{8}) \longrightarrow \frac{5}{8} \times \square \longrightarrow \frac{\triangle}{8} \longrightarrow \boxed{}$

d] $\frac{1}{2} + \frac{1}{2} + \frac{1}{2} + \frac{1}{2} + \frac{1}{2} \longrightarrow \square(\frac{1}{2}) \longrightarrow \frac{1}{2} \times \square \longrightarrow \frac{\triangle}{2} \longrightarrow \boxed{}$

4 Complete each matrix.

a]

Fraction	$\frac{8}{3}$	$\frac{11}{3}$				$\frac{17}{3}$		$\frac{22}{3}$	
Number of thirds	8			7	6		19		25
Mixed number	$2\frac{2}{3}$		$4\frac{1}{3}$			$5\frac{1}{3}$			

b]

Fraction	$\frac{7}{2}$		$\frac{9}{4}$						$\frac{19}{8}$
Numerator	7	11			29		43		
Denominator	2	5			6		8		
Mixed number	$3\frac{1}{2}$			$4\frac{1}{5}$		$7\frac{3}{4}$		$5\frac{1}{10}$	$2\frac{5}{12}$

MULTIPLICATION OF FRACTIONS

Their mother gives Ted, Joan, and Ruth $3\frac{1}{2}$ bars of chocolate each. The children want to find out how much chocolate their mother had to start with.

Ted uses this method.

$3(3\frac{1}{2}) = 3\frac{1}{2} + 3\frac{1}{2} + 3\frac{1}{2} = 3 + 3 + 3 + \frac{1}{2} + \frac{1}{2} + \frac{1}{2} = 9 + 1 + \frac{1}{2} = 10\frac{1}{2}$

Joan uses this method.

$3 \times 3\frac{1}{2} = 3 \times (3 + \frac{1}{2}) = (3 \times 3) + (3 \times \frac{1}{2}) = 9 + \frac{3}{2} = 9 + 1\frac{1}{2} = 10\frac{1}{2}$

Ruth uses this method.

$3 \times 3\frac{1}{2} = 3 \times \frac{7}{2} = \frac{21}{2} = 10\frac{1}{2}$

Their mother had $10\frac{1}{2}$ bars of chocolate.

We say the product of $3\frac{1}{2}$ and 3 is equivalent to the product of 3 and $3\frac{1}{2}$. The product is $10\frac{1}{2}$.

1   Use Ted's method to find the products.

a] $5(2\frac{1}{2})$ **b]** $2(3\frac{1}{3})$ **c]** $4(7\frac{3}{5})$ **d]** $3(4\frac{1}{3})$ **e]** $6(6\frac{1}{4})$ **f]** $7(1\frac{2}{3})$

2   Use Joan's method to find the products.

a] $6 \times 2\frac{1}{2}$ **b]** $7 \times 3\frac{1}{4}$ **c]** $9\frac{2}{3} \times 8$ **d]** $5\frac{1}{2} \times 2$ **e]** $8 \times 10\frac{3}{4}$ **f]** $3\frac{3}{4} \times 4$

3   Use Ruth's method to find the products.

a] $3 \times 4\frac{1}{2}$ **b]** $7\frac{2}{3} \times 6$ **c]** $5 \times 2\frac{1}{4}$ **d]** $9\frac{1}{3} \times 8$ **e]** $10 \times 7\frac{4}{5}$ **f]** $7 \times 6\frac{1}{2}$

4   Use any method to complete each matrix. Check the products you find by using a different method.

a]

Number	5	9	7	8	3	5	9	4	6	8
Mixed number	$3\frac{1}{2}$	$3\frac{1}{3}$	$4\frac{2}{5}$	$9\frac{3}{4}$	$6\frac{1}{2}$	$3\frac{1}{5}$	$7\frac{2}{3}$	$7\frac{1}{2}$	$8\frac{5}{6}$	$9\frac{1}{5}$
Product	$17\frac{1}{2}$									

b]

Mixed number	$7\frac{2}{3}$	$3\frac{2}{5}$	$2\frac{1}{3}$	$5\frac{1}{7}$	$8\frac{1}{4}$	$11\frac{1}{3}$	$12\frac{1}{2}$	$3\frac{2}{5}$	$9\frac{3}{5}$	$8\frac{3}{14}$
Number	3	4	5	7	9	6	8	10	9	7
Product										

FRACTION SITUATIONS

1 Half the people inside the supermarket at 10.00 hours on Saturday are women and one third of the people are men. The rest are children.

a] What fraction of the people are children?

b] How many children are there if there are 24 women?

2 Complete the matrix about the people inside the supermarket later in the day.

Time	11.00	12.00	13.00	14.00	15.00	16.00	17.00
Fraction that are women	$\frac{7}{12}$	$\frac{1}{2}$		$\frac{1}{2}$	$\frac{2}{3}$	$\frac{4}{7}$	
Fraction that are men	$\frac{1}{3}$	$\frac{2}{5}$			$\frac{1}{5}$	$\frac{2}{7}$	
Fraction that are children	$\frac{1}{12}$			$\frac{1}{8}$			$\frac{1}{10}$
Number of women	42	60					36
Number of men	24		6		12	24	
Number of children	6		4				6
Total number of people	72		24	40			

3 Complete, then total the bills.

a] 2½ kg of sugar ☐p
3½ kg of potatoes ☐p
5 eggs ☐p
1½ litres of vinegar ☐p
☐p

b] ½ kg of cheese ☐p
8 eggs ☐p
200 g of butter ☐p
2½ kg of flour ☐p
☐p

c] 6 oranges ☐p
200 g of bacon ☐p
3½ litres of milk ☐p
½ kg of sugar ☐p
☐p

d] 2 litres of milk ☐p
5½ kg of potatoes ☐p
350 g of bacon ☐p
250 g of cheese ☐p
☐p

4 Angela's mother buys 2½ m of material to make a dress and 3½ m to make a coat. The dress material costs £1·30 a metre. The coat material costs £2·42 a metre. How much did she pay altogether?

Section 10 · Measurement: Area

SELECTING A UNIT

The children are discussing ways of finding the area measurement of the surface of the front cover of Julie's book. They all agree they need a unit with the property of area to measure area.
Julie uses a disc. She records:

My unit is a disc.
I used 15 discs. The measure is 15.
The area measurement is approximately 15 disc units.

1   Tom, Dick, and Mary use different units. Record their measurements.

 Tom   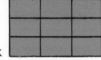 Dick   Mary

2   a]   Did Julie's discs cover the whole of the surface of the front cover?
b]   Is a disc a suitable unit for measuring area?

3   a]   Did Tom's equilateral triangular regions cover the whole of the surface of the front cover?
b]   If Tom had used some half equilateral triangular regions to fill in the spaces, what would he have recorded?
c]   Is an equilateral triangular region a suitable unit for measuring area?

4   a]   Why are rectangular regions and square regions more suitable units for measuring area than equilateral triangular regions?
b]   Why are square regions more suitable for measuring area than rectangular regions?

5   Find the area measurement of one surface of your book using as your unit:

     a]   a disc.   b]   an equilateral triangular region.
     c]   a rectangular region.   d]   a square region.

   Record your results.

My unit	Number of units	Measure	Area measurement

6   Using a centimetre square as your unit, find the area measurement of one surface of each of 6 objects. Record your results.

Surface of object	Selected unit	Measure	Area measurement
Small box	cm²	16	16 cm²

AREA OF RECTANGULAR REGIONS

Alan's father has still to tile part of the surface of one bathroom wall.
He calculates the number of tiles he will need: "There are 24 tiles in each row and 10 rows, 24 × 10 = 240. I will need 240 tiles."

Alan says: "The area measurement of the surface you have still to cover is 240 tile units."

1 Complete the matrix.

Number of tiles in each row	24	34	28	22	36	27	33	29
Number of rows	10	12	14	18	15	11	13	16
Number of tiles that will be needed	240							
Area measurement	240 tile units							

Susan calculates the area measurement of a rectangular region using centimetre squares. She records:

The base of the rectangular region is 4 cm.
The number of squares along the base is 4.
The height of the rectangular region is 2 cm.
The number of squares along the height is 2.
The total number of centimetre squares is 4 × 2 = 8.
The measure of the area is 8. The area measurement is (4 × 2) cm² = 8 cm².

2 Use Susan's method to calculate the area measurement of each of these rectangular regions.

Base	6 cm	9 cm	12 cm	26 cm	37 cm	18 cm	45 cm	52 cm
Height	5 cm	8 cm	7 cm	17 cm	23 cm	13 cm	25 cm	29 cm
Number of squares along base	6							
Number of squares along height	5							
Measure of the area	30							
Area measurement	30 cm²							

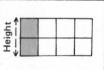

3 Play the Make a Square Game.

CALCULATING AREA

Steve partitions the rectangular region into strips 1 cm wide to help him calculate its area.

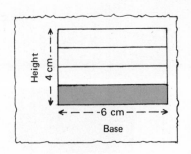

He records:

The height of the rectangle is 4 cm.
The number of strips is 4.
The base measures 6 cm.
The height of a strip is 1 cm.
The measure of the area of 1 strip is 6.
The area of 1 strip is 6 cm².
The area of the rectangular region is (4 × 6) cm² = 24 cm².

1

Use Steve's method to calculate the area of each of these rectangular regions.

Base (cm)	24	36	35	26	48	52	50	26	52	47	42	36	40
Height (cm)	18	24	27	13	18	13	13	25	50	23	28	22	16
Area (cm²)	432												

2

Calculate the area of each of these regions by partitioning each into rectangular regions.

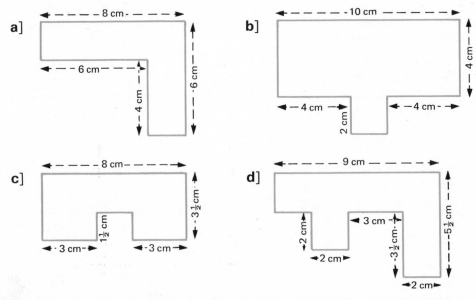

3

Check each of your results for Exercise 2 by calculating the area in a different way.

4

Draw some shapes which can be partitioned into rectangular regions.
Calculate the area of each region.

AREA OF TRIANGULAR REGIONS

You will need a geoboard and elastic bands.

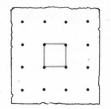

Use an elastic band to form this square region on a geoboard.
Use the square region as your selected unit.
We will call it one square unit.

1 Use elastic bands to form these regions.

a] ABUP b] ABP c] ABQ d] ABR
e] ABS   f] ABT g] ABU

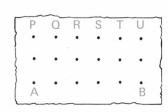

2 Calculate and record in square units the area of each region you formed in Exercise 1.

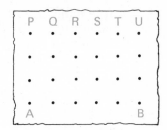

Region	ABUP	ABP	ABQ	ABR	ABS	ABT	ABU
Area (square units)							

3 a] What do you notice about the area of each triangular region in Exercise 2?
b] Compare the areas of rectangular region ABUP and triangular region ABP. What do you notice?

4 Repeat Exercises 1–3 using a geoboard marked in this way.

5 Repeat Exercises 1–3 using a geoboard marked in this way.

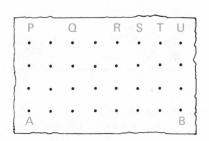

AREA: PROPERTIES OF TRIANGLES

You will need several rectangular pieces of card.

1   Label vertices B and C and mark a point A on the edge opposite $\overline{BC}$.
Form $\overline{AB}$ and $\overline{AC}$.

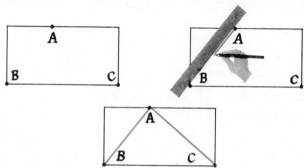

2   Cut along $\overline{AB}$ and $\overline{AC}$.

a] Can you cover triangle ABC using the other two triangles?
b] What relationship do you notice between the area of triangular region ABC and the area of the face of the card?

3   Using other rectangular pieces of card, repeat the experiment marking point A in different positions on the edge. Is the relationship still true?

4   Using centimetre squared paper, copy triangle DEF and points P, S, R, and Q.

5   Cut out triangle DEF. What do you notice about the lengths of:
a] $\overline{DP}$ and $\overline{EP}$?   **b]** $\overline{DR}$ and $\overline{FR}$?

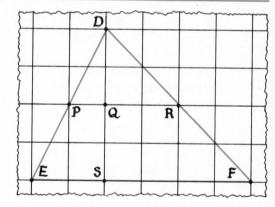

6   Draw $\overline{PR}$ and $\overline{DQ}$. Cut out triangles DPQ and DQR, leaving shape EPRF.

7   **a]** Using the shapes DPQ, DQR, and EPRF, form a rectangle.
b] What relationship do you notice between the area of the rectangular region you have just formed and the area of triangular region DEF?

8   Repeat Exercises 4–7 using a triangle DEF with these length measurements: $\overline{ES}$ 4 cm, $\overline{SF}$ 6 cm, and $\overline{DS}$ 8 cm.

BASES AND HEIGHTS OF TRIANGLES

Mike and Joy are arguing about which side of a triangle is called the base. When their teacher overhears them, she says: "You can look at a triangle from three different directions."

From their teacher's direction, the base is $\overline{BC}$.
From Joy's direction, the base is $\overline{AB}$.
From Mike's direction, the base is $\overline{AC}$.

1 Look at each triangle from these directions. Record which side is the base.

a] 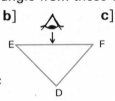   b]   c]   d]   e]

2 Draw each of these triangles and record a base. Then draw in an eye to show from which direction you looked.

a] 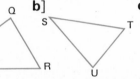   b]    c]   d] 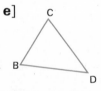   e]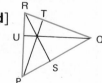

c]

Next Mike and Joy argue about how to find the height of a triangle. Their teacher says: "There are three different heights. You can find each height by using a set square. Draw a line segment from a vertex to a base, so that the base is perpendicular to the line segment."

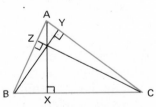

Their teacher records:
When the base is $\overline{BC}$, the height is $\overline{AX}$.
When the base is $\overline{AB}$, the height is $\overline{CZ}$.
When the base is $\overline{AC}$, the height is $\overline{BY}$.

3 Record in the same way as the teacher the three different heights for each of these triangles.

a]   b]   c]   d]

AREA OF TRIANGULAR REGIONS

Martin draws a triangle APB on centimetre squared paper. To help him calculate the area of the triangular region, he draws a rectangle ADCB around it as shown.

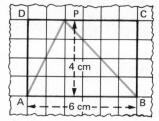

Martin knows the area of triangular region APB is half the area of rectangular region ADCB. He knows the base of the triangle APB is equal to the base of the rectangle ADCB. He knows the height of the triangle APB is equal to the height of the rectangle ADCB. Because the area of rectangular region ADCB is (6 × 4) cm² = 24 cm², the area of triangular region APB is $\frac{1}{2}$(24) cm² = 12 cm².

1   Use Martin's method to calculate the area of each of these triangular regions. Use centimetre squared paper to help if you wish.

a]

b]

c]

d]

e]

Rachel calculates the area of Martin's triangular region using this method.

She knows the area of triangular region APB is equal to the area of rectangular region AXYB.

The base of rectangle AXYB is the same as the base of triangle APB.
The height of rectangle AXYB is half the height of triangle APB.
The area of rectangular region AXYB is (6 × 2) cm² = 12 cm².
The area of triangular region APB is 12 cm².

2   Use Rachel's method to calculate the area of each of these triangular regions.

a]

b]

c]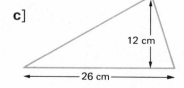

d]

60

ENRICHMENT

Andrew wants to calculate the area of region ABCDE.

He draws $\overline{BE}$ to partition the region into two regions.

Rectangular region BCDE has an area of
(5×4) cm² = 20 cm².

Triangular region ABE has an area of
$(\frac{1}{2} \times 4 \times 2)$ cm² = 4 cm².

The total area of region ABCDE is $(20 + 4)$ cm² = 24 cm².

1 Calculate the area of each of these regions.

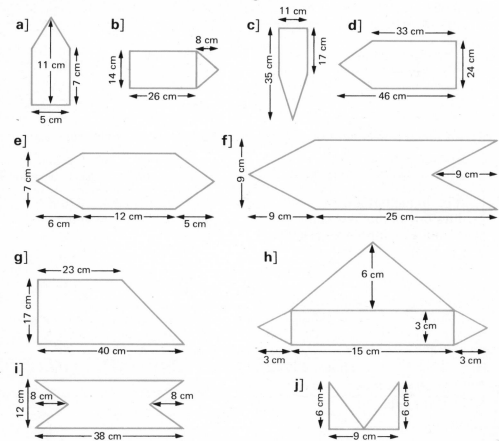

2 Play the Triangular Region Game.

Section 11 · Enrichment

AT THE CAR SHOWROOM

The performance and cost of each car in the showroom is given in the matrix.

Car	A	B	C	D	E	F	G
Maximum speed (kph)	132	168	162	222	276	152	120
Overall fuel consumption (litres per 100 km)	9·4	10·5	12·8	14·0	20·1	11·7	7·0
Cost	£956	£1242	£2601	£3971	£9572	£1587	£727

1 Calculate the amount of money taken if the salesman sells these cars.

a] A and B   b] C and D   c] D and G   d] E and F
e] C, E, and G   f] D, B, and F   g] A, G, and D   h] C, F, and G

2 A customer has a car to trade-in. The salesman offers him £575 if he buys one of the new cars in the showroom. Calculate how much he would pay for each of these cars.

a] A   b] B   c] C   d] D   e] E   f] F   g] G

3 Another customer has no car to trade-in but wishes to pay cash. The salesman offers him a discount of $\frac{1}{10}$ off the price of the car.
Complete the matrix showing the discount and cash price for each car.

Car	A	B	C	D	E	F	G
Cost	£956	£1242	£2601	£3971	£9572	£1587	£727
$\frac{1}{10}$ discount							
Cash price							

4 Record on a separate bar chart the data about:

a] the maximum speed of each car in kilometres per hour.
b] the overall fuel consumption of each car in litres per 100 km.

AT THE CAR SHOWROOM

1   Calculate the median maximum speed for:

     a] the 3 most expensive cars.   **b]** the 3 least expensive cars.
     c] all the 7 cars.

2   Repeat Exercises 1 a] and b] for the mean instead of the median
     maximum speed.

3   **a]** Complete the matrix showing the volume of petrol in litres each car
     would use for these journeys.

Car	A	B	C	D	E	F	G
100 km							
200 km							
400 km							
600 km							
800 km							
1000 km							

     b] Check each of your results in the matrix using a different method.

4   Calculate the floor area of the car showroom.

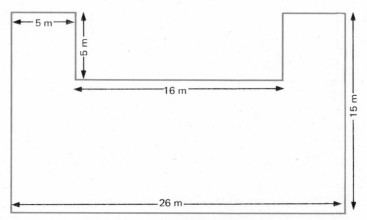

5   The floor area of the showroom is covered by tiles, each measuring
     25 cm × 25 cm.
     Calculate the number of tiles required to cover:

     a] 1 square metre of the floor area.   **b]** the total floor area.

6   Calculate the cost of the tiles required to cover the total floor area when
     each tile costs 15p.

MORE ABOUT CARS

1 Complete the matrix showing the cost of replacing tyres on each car.

Car	A	B	C	D	E	F	G
1 tyre	£9·52	£12·75	£16·43	£19·74	£25·90	£10·75	£7·71
2 tyres							
3 tyres							
4 tyres							
5 tyres							

2 Calculate the annual cost of running this car. The car licence costs £25 a year, insurance charges are £47·25, depreciation is £136, repairs and maintenance cost £57·80. The car travels 10,000 km a year using petrol, which costs 9p per litre, at the mean rate of 8·2 litres per 100 km.

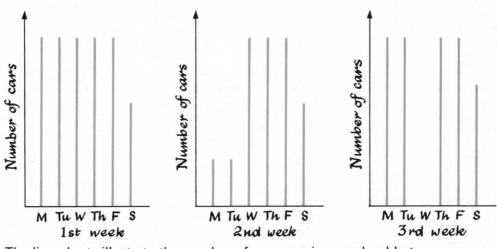

3 The line charts illustrate the number of cars passing a school between 08.30 hours and 09.00 hours from Monday to Saturday in three separate weeks. Can you give a reasonable explanation for the volume of traffic on:

a] Saturday of the 1st week?
b] Monday and Tuesday of the 2nd week?
c] Wednesday of the 3rd week?

4 a] Make a tally of the favourite car of each child in your class.
b] Record your findings on a bar chart.
c] Which is the most popular model?
d] What do you think are the reasons for its popularity?
e] On a matrix, show the cost and maximum speed of each of the different makes of car illustrated on your bar chart.

BOOK 5 · CONTENTS

Printed in Spain by Mateu-Cromo, Artes Gráficas, S.A.

GHJKL 798765